PENGUIN PASSNOTES

The Long and the Short and the T

Maureen Blakesley was born in Staffordshire and educated at the University of Keele. She is at present Head of the English Department at Longdean School, Hemel Hempstead, Hertfordshire. She is also the author of the study guide to *Hobson's Choice* in the Penguin Passnotes series.

PENGUIN PASSNOTES

WILLIS HALL

The Long and the Short and the Tall

MAUREEN BLAKESLEY, M.A.

ADVISORY EDITOR: STEPHEN COOTE, M.A., PH.D.

PENGUIN BOOKS

PENGUIN BOOKS

Published by the Penguin Group

27 Wrights Lane, London W8 5TZ, England

Viking Penguin Inc., 40 West 23rd Street, New York, New York 10010, USA

Penguin Books Australia Ltd, Ringwood, Victoria, Australia

Penguin Books Canada Ltd, 2801 John Street, Markham, Ontario, Canada L3R 1B4

Penguin Books (NZ) Ltd, 182–190 Wairau Road, Auckland 10, New Zealand

Penguin Books Ltd, Registered Offices: Harmondsworth, Middlesex, England

First published 1989

Made and printed in Great Britain by

Richard Clay Ltd, Bungay, Suffolk

Filmset in Monophoto Ehrhardt

Contents

To the Student

The purpose of this book is to help you to understand and appreciate Willis Hall's play *The Long and the Short and the Tall*. It will help you to follow what happens in the play and why the characters speak and behave as they do. When you have thought about this behaviour and about the themes which run through the play, you should be able to enjoy it more.

You will need to read the play through carefully, perhaps several times if you are to know it really well. Unlike a novel, the whole purpose of a play is to be acted on stage in front of an audience. If you are able to see the play, then being a member of the audience is quite a different experience from reading the text. But if you cannot attend a performance of the play, you will have to use your imagination to see the characters on stage for yourself. Perhaps you could read it through or act it out with friends. Acting a part is one of the best ways of understanding the playwright's intention because you have to understand thoroughly the character you are playing in order to convince someone else of his reality.

You may be able to see the film which was made of the play in 1960 and had Richard Todd in the role of Sergeant Mitchem. Or you may see a repeat of the BBC version of the play in which Mark McManus played Mitchem and Michael Kitchen played Bamforth. Both of these versions differed in some detail from the text we have. You might ask yourself why the directors chose to alter the details and especially the ending of the play.

A combination of all these ways of experiencing the play would help you to form your own opinions about it. Different interpretations will show that there is no absolute answer to the way it should be staged and that your opinions about the play, provided you can always support them with evidence from the text, are just as valid as the opinions of anyone else.

This Passnote has been written to help you form your own opinions by asking yourself questions. Why does the playwright emphasize certain themes? Why do the characters behave and speak as they do? Why is this play so important to us today even though the events it depicts took place nearly fifty years ago? You will probably be able to think of other questions which are important to you when you know the play thoroughly.

When you are familiar with this play and have worked through many of the questions – answering them in written form, in discussion or in dramatic work – you will be able to write persuasively and confidently about it.

Background to the Play

THE PLAYWRIGHT

Willis Hall was born in Leeds in 1929. At seventeen he joined the professional army, which took him for several years to the Far East, where he began writing for Radio Malaya.

He has written many plays for radio, television and the theatre. This play, *The Long and the Short and the Tall*, was first produced in 1958 at the Edinburgh Festival under the title *The Disciplines of War*. It was later produced at the Royal Court Theatre and then transferred to the New Theatre with great success.

Willis Hall has also collaborated with another writer, Keith Waterhouse, to write the stage play *Billy Liar*, which later became a successful film. Other film scripts include *Whistle Down the Wind* and *A Kind of Loving*. For the theatre they have written *All Things Bright and Beautiful*, *Celebration*, *Say Who You Are*, *Children's Day* and *Who's Who?*.

Willis Hall has written extensively about sport and contributes a weekly column to the *Yorkshire Evening Post*. He has also written several children's books, including *The Return of the Antelope*, *Dragon Days*, *The Inflatable Shop*, *The Last Vampire* and *The Summer of the Dinosaur*.

Willis Hall's plays and novels have proved popular because of their realism and their believable characters. *The Long and the Short and the Tall* is no exception.

HISTORICAL BACKGROUND

Willis Hall has set his play in the Malayan Peninsula during the Second World War, at the time when the Japanese forces were pouring south to surprise the British forces garrisoning Singapore, an important port in Malaysia. Singapore was fortified in the belief that an attack would come from the sea; so the attack from the north was totally unexpected. The British forces were easily defeated and Singapore was occupied by the Japanese until the Japanese surrender at the end of the war. Willis Hall was one of those British soldiers and stayed on to work in Singapore after the war. He is writing from first-hand experience.

If you would like to know more about the war in the Far East and, in particular, the Japanese occupation of Singapore, your local library will have books to help you.

THE TITLE OF THE PLAY

The title is taken from a song popular with soldiers during the Second World War. The full song is printed in your play-text on pages xxi and xxii. It puts forward the position of the ordinary soldier, the private, against the NCOs who order ordinary soldiers about all the time and give them hell. It has some humour and affection as does Willis Hall's play and above all it shows how ordinary men will triumph over the horrors of war and the petty rules of the army. It is about *all* the soldiers – The Long and the Short and the Tall. The song and the play illustrate the universal experience of ordinary men caught up in the army and in war. Most of all, the song emphasizes hope: 'So cheer up, my lads, bless 'em all'. The play turns this hope upside down with its sad ending in which most of the soldiers die. This is the irony of the title.

Synopsis

ACT ONE

Willis Hall's play *The Long and the Short and the Tall* is set in a deserted hut in the Malayan jungle. The time is early 1942 just as the Japanese Imperial Army is about to sweep down the peninsula taking Singapore from the rear.

The scene is set by the noise of heavy gunfire in the distance, 'the chirruping of crickets and the song of a bird in the jungle'. The first character seen by the audience is Corporal Johnstone who cautiously inspects the room, kicks the door open and then beckons a colleague to follow him. This man is Sergeant Mitchem who then indicates to the rest of the patrol they should follow him.

Five soldiers run into the room. The stage-direction tells us that they are 'tired and dishevelled' and that they 'stack their rifles in a corner of the hut and sit gratefully on the floor'. Almost immediately the audience can tell important information about the group. From their 'stripes' Mitchem is a sergeant, Johnstone a corporal and Macleish a lance-corporal. One of them, Whitaker, carries a radio-transmitter on his back. All of them are armed; the two senior soldiers have sten-guns.

Immediately one of the patrol, Bamforth, gains the attention of the audience by lying out and making himself comfortable and thereby arousing the anger of Johnstone, the corporal. He has taken off his back-pack before being given permission by the sergeant and it is clear that he has been, and perhaps will continue to be, a trouble-maker.

We learn too that the radio-transmitter is virtually useless because of a flat battery. In order to establish their surroundings, and presumably whether there are any Japanese forces nearby, the two senior NCOs, Mitchem and Johnstone, leave the hut, allowing the men half an hour's rest before they attempt the trek back to base.

While they are away, the audience sees more of the rest of the patrol, especially Bamforth who teases and then wrestles with Evans, and then has a fairly serious squabble with Macleish, the lance-corporal. We also witness Whitaker's attempts to raise a signal from base-camp on the failing radio-set and the way in which Bamforth teases him over his failure. The Welsh private, Evans, seems in good spirits but is also taunted by Bamforth about the women's magazine sent to him by his mother. We learn a little about the men's home lives, particularly about Evans and his Welsh girlfriend, and about Smith who is married with two children. Smith reminisces about his council house and the gardening he has done there. Gradually the audience learns to distinguish between the members of the patrol.

Bamforth's teasing of Evans eventually descends into a mock fight in which Bamforth twists Evans's leg until he confesses that he is an 'ignorant Welsh Taff'. The noise from this scuffle partly drowns the radio-transmitter which is being operated by Whitaker. He insists that he heard voices but too much interference drowned out any message.

All of this banter between Bamforth and the others eventually becomes too much for the patience of Macleish who has been left in charge and clearly is under some stress. They are obviously getting ready to fight – and this is not the good-natured kind of tussle which Bamforth and Evans had indulged in earlier. This scrap takes away the attention of the men on guard duty and into the midst of this return Mitchem and Johnstone. Mitchem is not pleased that the discipline of the patrol should have collapsed in his absence. He responds by resorting to army discipline, bringing the men to attention as if for an inspection and asking the culprits to own up. It is only after the threat of punishment for all of them that Bamforth steps forward to admit his part in the squabble.

In the longest speech in the play, Mitchem first of all gives Bamforth a sound telling-off, warning him that he, Mitchem, is more than a match for all Bamforth's trouble-making, and secondly Mitchem outlines to the rest of the patrol his plan for getting them all back to base-camp. This reminder of the proximity of the Japanese prompts Macleish to admit to his worry about his brother who is with a

Scottish regiment further up-country, nearer to the enemy front-lines.

Whitaker is still sporadically trying the radio-set for any contact with base-camp and eventually, the stage-directions tell us, a 'faint murmur of speech can be heard from the set'. They all soon understand that this speech is not from the British army but from the Japanese and that, with such a weak battery in the set, the range can be only a few miles. The realization that the Japanese are so near worries them all but especially Macleish whose brother is with the 'forward' troops.

Mitchem's reaction to this is to try to restore their confidence by making light of their worries. He admits that there is a possibility that the Japanese army has broken through but tries to persuade them that it is more likely to be a small patrol, rather like themselves, and that the Japanese patrol will be as worried as his group is. At the same time he asks Johnstone to check the sten-guns and is clearly planning to move out of the hut immediately. He gives orders that the men should get their back-packs on and that Johnstone should lead the way back, as quickly as possible.

This preparation is interrupted by Bamforth who is on sentry-duty at the window. He thinks he sees movement on the track about fifty yards away. The movement turns out to be a Japanese soldier who has slipped away to smoke a cigarette. Instead of returning, the enemy soldier discovers the track leading to the hut and moves towards them. Bamforth would have shot him except that Mitchem knocks the rifle out of aiming position. He is worried that a rifle shot would betray their position.

When it is clear that the Japanese soldier is going to investigate the hut, the whole patrol hides under the windows hoping that he will not see them. However, Whitaker has left the radio-transmitter on the table in full view of anyone looking through the window, and it is this which makes the Japanese investigate the hut further.

As he comes through the door, he is grabbed by Johnstone who puts a hand over his mouth and holds him firmly asking for one of the others to kill the prisoner. All of them, except Bamforth, refuse to stab the Japanese with a bayonet and, just as Bamforth is about to do so, Mitchem dashes back into the hut from the veranda where he has been surveying the forest for any other enemy soldiers.

Mitchem wants to keep the prisoner alive and speaks to him in pidgin English to try to explain this. He wants the prisoner to keep quiet, otherwise Bamforth will bayonet him. The prisoner soon understands this. When he is released from Johnstone's hold and they all look at him they see that he is heavily armed with a revolver, grenades and a bayonet. Bamforth disarms him and is given the task of guarding him, which he does with a bayonet. Immediately, Bamforth takes the opportunity to speak pidgin English himself saying that he is teaching the prisoner to put his hands on his head and down again.

Johnstone and Mitchem, meanwhile, discuss the possibility of taking the prisoner back to camp with them. They both know it is a risk but Mitchem is prepared to take it. In order to prepare for their exit again, Mitchem sends Macleish and Smith out to reconnoitre the path as far as the main track. While they are away, Mitchem explains why he wants to take the prisoner back to base-camp. He thinks that the prisoner will be able to divulge useful information about the strength of the Japanese army. Any trouble from the prisoner on the trek back would mean that Mitchem would bayonet him himself.

The Japanese prisoner is becoming more relaxed and shows Bamforth photographs of his wife and family. In return Bamforth gives the prisoner one of his cigarettes, an action which makes Johnstone very angry. The two squabble and Bamforth attacks Johnstone with the result that Mitchem puts Bamforth on a charge, under open arrest. Before things can go further, Smith and Macleish return with bad news. They have seen hundreds of Japanese soldiers pouring down the main track, clearly having broken through the British forward line. They have managed to cover up the entrance to the path leading to the hut.

Mitchem's response is that his patrol must make their way across country to warn the British at base-camp of the Japanese breakthrough. Johnstone disagrees and also asks what will happen to the prisoner now that the situation has changed. Mitchem's reply is a quick, 'We're ditching him' before he turns to Whitaker asking him to try the radio once more. This Whitaker does, and the response is a

Japanese radio-operator's voice saying 'Johnee! We–you–come–to–get.' The horror of this dawns on all of them; they all turn to look at the Japanese prisoner who, not understanding, performs his party-trick of putting his hands on his head.

The curtain falls.

ACT TWO

This scene is exactly the same as for Act One and the time is thirty minutes later.

Smith and Whitaker are still on duty at the windows, Macleish is guarding the Japanese prisoner, Mitchem is cleaning his sten-gun and the other three members of the patrol are asleep. Whitaker is clearly jumpy and worried; a stage-direction tells us that he 'starts and raises his rifle' when a bird sings out in the jungle. He also asks Mitchem the time, telling a story to Smith about when his own watch was stolen, and then asks Mitchem the time again. He is clearly desperate to be relieved from guard-duty so that he can relax and sleep.

Mitchem allows the prisoner a drink of water and Macleish takes this opportunity to start a discussion about him. He thinks the Japanese prisoner isn't 'a bad sort of bloke' and that he is 'a family man himself'. This gives Mitchem the opportunity to philosophize about killing the enemy and also to air his views that what is wrong with the world is women – or 'bints' as he calls them. It is women, he says, who encourage a man to join the army and feel patriotic and in a few weeks he is dead. So Macleish should forget that the prisoner has a home and family or he 'might end up like him'.

Macleish has suspected that the prisoner will be left behind and questions Mitchem carefully about it. He seems slow to understand that Mitchem intends to kill the prisoner and, even when he does, he tries to argue that the prisoner should be left alive but tied up. His argument is that the Japanese soldier is a prisoner of war and therefore should not be killed. Macleish is thinking of his own younger brother who is probably in a similar situation to their prisoner. Mitchem knows that strictly speaking Macleish is right but is prepared to defend the course of common sense against the rules of the 'book'. He knows too that Macleish will experience many more agonizing decisions about death, saying, 'If this war shapes the way I think it will, you'll grow up, lad, in next to no time.'

Again Whitaker interrupts, wanting to know the time. He is anxious to be relieved of guard-duty and this time Mitchem responds by waking up the three sleeping members of the patrol. Bamforth goes outside the hut for a few minutes to relieve himself and Johnstone again questions Mitchem about the prisoner and the way he is to be killed. It is clear that Johnstone would like to do the killing himself.

Johnstone notices that the Japanese prisoner is smoking and, when he investigates, he discovers that the cigarettes are British. Mitchem jumps to the obvious conclusion: the Japanese has been looting. Johnstone is infuriated by this thought and is all in favour of beating up the prisoner there and then. Macleish again remembers his younger brother, only just nineteen, who might have been the very British soldier from whom the cigarettes were looted. When they go through the prisoner's pockets, Johnstone takes the opportunity to tear up the photographs of the Japanese man's wife and children.

Into the middle of all this Bamforth returns and is astounded by what he sees. He tells them that he gave the cigarettes to the Japanese prisoner. He had not looted them. This news stops the attack on the prisoner and Bamforth is disgusted with their behaviour. To try to make amends, Evans picks up the torn pieces of the photographs and tries to explain that they can be stuck back together again.

It is Johnstone who will not let the matter rest. He insists on inspecting the prisoner's cigarette-case and discovers that it was made in Birmingham. Again Bamforth comes to the defence of the prisoner explaining that he might well have bought the cigarette-case; he has not necessarily looted it. In order to strengthen his case he cites Whitaker who, apparently, has an enormous stock of Japanese goods – buttons, cap badges, belts and so on. Whitaker is extremely embarrassed by this revelation and tries to explain away his stock of Japanese goods as 'souvenirs'. Although Macleish in particular is not convinced by Bamforth's argument, it does put a stop to further accusations of looting by the Japanese prisoner.

Again Whitaker asks the time; he is clearly impatient to be relieved of guard-duty and this time Mitchem responds by replacing him with Macleish. Evans replaces Smith as the other guard. Whitaker decides to fill his time by reading the women's magazine belonging to Evans and is again teased by Bamforth who says he is not old enough to read such things and is 'pig-ignorant'. This teasing reminds Whitaker of his girlfriend at home and he tells the other men about her and how he used to take her out. The story is moving and even Bamforth is quiet. Whitaker reflects that the girl no longer writes to him and is comforted by Smith who tells him that the mail has probably been held up.

The light outside begins to dim and the men fall quiet. Bamforth sings a mournful song, an army song about a dying soldier. Yet again Mitchem encourages them to get packed and ready for the journey back to base-camp. He has been waiting for darkness.

The question of the Japanese prisoner arises again when Bamforth offers him a drink from his water-bottle. Johnstone immediately interferes and is supported by Mitchem who eventually has to confess to Bamforth that the prisoner will not be going with them. Johnstone picks up the Japanese bayonet from the table and Bamforth stands in front of the prisoner to protect him, refusing to obey Mitchem's commands to move. No one else in the patrol supports Bamforth's defence of the prisoner and Mitchem orders Whitaker to cover the prisoner with a sten-gun. When Mitchem and Johnstone move forward to overpower Bamforth, the prisoner rises to his feet, not understanding what is going on. Whitaker's terror causes his finger to tighten on the trigger and the prisoner dies in a hail of bullets from the sten-gun. Whitaker is terrified by what he has done.

Mitchem immediately realizes that the noise has pinpointed their position to the Japanese forces outside and that their only hope is to move quickly and try to get away. He orders Johnstone to have one last try at the radio-transmitter before they leave, but the set is dead. There is no response.

One by one the members of the patrol leave the hut and, as the stage empties, the audience can hear the British army operator replying on the radio. Almost immediately a machine-gun clatters outside and we hear the screams of dying men. The door is pushed open and Johnstone, wounded, staggers back into the hut. He hears the operator on the radio but shouts insults into the handset and then switches it off.

The play ends with Johnstone crawling over to the body of the Japanese prisoner, smoking one of his cigarettes, and then, taking the prisoner's white scarf, tying it around the barrel of his sten. He waves the white flag at the window.

The curtain falls.

Commentary on the Plot

(The page references are taken from the Heinemann edition 1965.)

The stage-directions set the scene very precisely. The audience is watching a 'wooden-walled, palm-thatched, dingy interior of a deserted store-hut in the Malayan jungle'. There are windows and a door in the far wall and the hut contains a rickety table, two chairs and a form. The sounds we hear also set the scene – gunfire, crickets and a bird.

The play's first performance in the 1950s was much nearer in time to the historical events that form the background of the play – the Japanese advance down the Malayan peninsula, culminating in the fall of the British stronghold of Singapore. But even then it was necessary to inform the audience of the precise timing of the play. Programme notes are important but not all members of an audience read these. The director of this play for the English Stage Company in January 1959, Lindsay Anderson, set the scene even more precisely. 'In the London production we placed the situation historically by a further device: we opened, as the houselights faded, with a solo verse, followed by a chorus, of the song from which the play takes its title. On the last line of this we mixed into the voice of a BBC announcer delivering a typical news bulletin of the period. This conveyed the information that Singapore was still held by the British ("rumours of a plan to evacuate the base have been authoritatively . . .") and that the situation on the mainland was quiet ("minor patrol activity continues"). As the announcer started a fresh paragraph ("Listeners at home are reminded that the new clothing rationing period starts on Tuesday"), his voice faded away mixing into a jungle bird-call and the sound of crickets.'

Now we are even further removed from the events of the Second World War and even fewer of the audience would know the details of the Japanese army's advance in Malaya.

How important is it that the audience should have a clear picture of the historical background of the play? If you were directing this play, how would you set the scene? Remember that your audience has to understand the situation and you have only a few minutes of sound-effects to do this. What would you put in the programme notes for your production? Would you use extracts from a history text book, maps of the area, or what?

The second problem to overcome is for the audience to understand exactly what is the role of each of the characters as they come on-stage. In the 1950s men over eighteen had to serve two years' National Service in the armed forces. The Second World War was not very far away in the past and there were many films made about the war. Most of the audience then would recognize from the 'stripes' on their arms that Mitchem with three stripes was a sergeant, the senior NCO, and therefore in charge, that Johnstone with two stripes was a corporal and therefore second-in-command and that Macleish, with one stripe, was a lance-corporal. None of the other men had any stripes and were thus ordinary private soldiers. How would you make sure that your audience understood the distinctions in rank between the soldiers? Would you use programme notes or would you presume that everyone immediately understood? Write a paragraph for your programme explaining these various ranks.

Much of the dialogue of the play is in army jargon and 1940s slang. What would you do to ensure that your audience understood the language? Would you alter any of it?

ACT ONE

When the seven men of the patrol burst into the hut they are all tired and dishevelled and are clearly looking for somewhere to take shelter and rest. The audience can clearly see that the patrol is prepared to meet hostile forces because the men are armed with rifles, and Mitchem and Johnstone have sten-guns. As soon as they are safely inside, one of the men sets up a radio-receiver on the table and starts trying to tune it in. It is clear that they are anxious to contact their base-camp but whether to impart information or just to establish communication, we do not yet know.

One of the men, Bamforth, immediately takes off his back-pack and settles down for a nap on the form. This action infuriates Johnstone, the corporal, and there are angry words between them.

Do you think Evans is right when he says to Bamforth, 'Johnno's got it in for you, boyo'? Why should this be so? Can you imagine what has been happening on this patrol before they get to the hut which makes the tension between them so great that they squabble immediately?

In this first encounter, the stage-instructions tell us that Bamforth 'glances across at Mitchem' who supports Johnstone by saying, 'You heard what he said.' Why do you think Bamforth does this? Later, of course, Mitchem has to intervene in their squabbling by saying, 'Right. Pack it in. That's both of you.'

What do you think Mitchem thinks about the way Johnstone and Bamforth behave?

Immediately this quarrel is stopped – for the moment – Mitchem sets about organizing the men. He asks two men to volunteer to guard the windows, sets Whitaker to keep trying the radio-set, tells the rest of the patrol to try to get some sleep and sets out with Johnstone on a quick reconnaissance in the immediate area.

What do you think are the worries going through Mitchem's mind? Make a list as if you were Mitchem thinking about all the possibilities. Remember that Mitchem does not know the end of the play as you may do. Put yourself in his position at the beginning of the play.

Because Johnstone and Mitchem leave the hut, Macleish, the lance-corporal, is left in charge. From what you have already seen of the way Bamforth behaves, what do you guess will be his attitude towards Macleish?

At first Bamforth spends his time teasing Evans and trying to prove that Londoners are tougher than Welshmen. Evans takes all this in good part and even joins him in some banter with Smith whose contribution to this discussion is, 'Why don't you jack it in?' They are clearly getting on Smith's nerves. Why do you think this is? Why should Smith be bad-tempered and touchy?

Eventually, Macleish, who is on guard at the other window from Smith, makes the same appeal: 'Bamforth, why don't you pack it in? We've heard about enough from you.'

This gives Bamforth the chance to turn his attention to Macleish and to be rude to him. The squabble gets quite heated and this time Smith intervenes to try to quieten things down, saying, 'Drop it, Mac. He didn't mean no harm.' This time, however, the squabble is continued by Evans who supports Bamforth in his baiting of Macleish.

Look at Macleish's reply on page 7, beginning 'It so happens that I accepted the rank of Lance-Corporal . . .' What kind of language is he using? Why does he speak like this? What does it tell us about him?

Bamforth, undaunted, having teased everyone in the room except Whitaker, now includes him in the insults, calling him 'Fanny Whitaker' and singing a song just when Whitaker thinks he is tuning the radio-set in to a station. This time it is Whitaker who repeats, 'Pack it in, Bamforth.'

What has Bamforth got against Whitaker? Why should he be so rude to him? Look again at pages 8 and 9 and the remarks which Bamforth makes about Whitaker. Do you think Bamforth always behaves like this or is he on edge, worried about their situation?

He is so rude to Whitaker that both Macleish and Smith are drawn into the argument. Evans defuses the situation slightly when he speaks, because Bamforth seems to be able to stand being teased by Evans whose sense of humour lightens the atmosphere.

The next episode concerns the women's magazine which Evans has in his pack, sent to him by his mother. Evans is following the serial which is a typical women's magazine love story, unreal and romantic. Both Smith and Bamforth are keen to borrow the magazine and Bamforth reads aloud one of the letters to the 'agony column'. Of course, he alters the magazine's reply so that he can make yet another insulting remark about corporals. This magazine would not seem to us to be of any interest to fighting soldiers. Why, then, do you think, are Smith and Bamforth so keen to borrow it? Does this episode tell us anything new about any of the characters?

The discussion about women and love, brought on by the magazine, leads Bamforth to tease Evans about his Welsh girlfriend. Evans has not seen her for eighteen months and Bamforth now tries to make him jealous by describing England during the war with all the girls going out with soldiers posted at home. Evans is confident that his girl at home is faithful to him or his mother would write and let him know. Why, do you think, does Bamforth try to unsettle Evans in this way? Is it kind?

Perhaps Bamforth realizes that he has gone rather too far because he tries to make a joke and bring Smith into the conversation. Macleish's reaction is, 'I fail to see, Bamforth, what experience you've had on the subject.' Why does he say that? What do you think of Bamforth's reply?

The playwright now takes the opportunity to fill in a little of the background about Smith who reminisces about his home and especially about his garden. What effect does this have on the audience? Do you think that getting to know a character better encourages you to have more sympathy for or understanding of that person?

Pause for a moment in your reading of the play and jot down your impressions so far of Bamforth, Evans, Smith and Macleish. Which of them do you like best and why?

The mention of homes and families gives Bamforth the opportunity to tease Evans once again about his Welsh girlfriend and to suggest that she has another boyfriend – one of the Allies. This leads to a scrap between them in which Bamforth wrestles Evans down to the floor, twists his foot and won't release him until he confesses 'I'm an ignorant Welsh Taff.' It is quite good-natured, like two small boys wrestling, but in the noise and confusion Whitaker believes that he can hear speech on the radio. The radio is loud enough for the audience to hear but not clear enough to distinguish what is being said. Evans, too, hears the voices. Bamforth tries to turn it into a joke, likening Evans to Joan of Arc (who also believed she heard voices – in her case God's voice telling her to lead an army against the English in fifteenth-century France).

Again Bamforth teases Whitaker about his inability to contact basecamp on the radio; in fact, he is quite rude to Whitaker, describing Whitaker's efforts as trying to impress Sergeant Mitchem. Why, do you think, does Bamforth do this? Is he right in his criticism of Whitaker's efforts? He says of Whitaker, 'You make me sick.' Do you think this is the effect Whitaker would have on the audience or would they feel more sympathetic towards him? Give your reasons.

Before Whitaker or anyone else can answer Bamforth, he changes the subject completely and starts to criticize the food in his ration-pack. When he says, 'I'll swing for that ration corporal one of these days,' he means that he will kill him and be hanged himself for punishment – a typical Bamforth exaggeration!

However, this change of subject by Bamforth does not deter the others from continuing to discuss and worry about the indistinct voices on the radio. The fact that Whitaker is unsure about whose voices they are is unsettling for us, the audience, too. He is, after all, the expert. What do you think the voices are? Why?

Smith shows his disillusion with the army and with the patrol when he describes their job as 'Playing at soldiers.' The same idea is taken up by Bamforth when he says, 'You can stick this for a game of soldiers,' describing their patrol as 'just about the crummiest detail in the Far East'. What do you think? Is it a 'crummy' patrol? What would make it less crummy?

In spite of the worrying voices on the radio-set, Whitaker chooses this moment to start darning his socks, an occupation which Bamforth immediately ridicules. He takes the opportunity to show how different he is from the rest of the men in the patrol by describing how he will escape 'when the Japs get here'. Without anyone actually saying so, it is clear that they all expect the Japanese army to arrive any moment. Bamforth, using a mock American accent, describes his intended escape as if he is narrating a travelogue – the kind of film which they all would have seen at the cinema. He intends, he says, to disguise himself as a native and escape, while 'the invading army of the Rising Sun is carving pieces out of Private Whitaker.'

Bamforth's teasing of Whitaker once more brings Macleish into the squabble. Macleish becomes even more angry when Bamforth then criticizes 'two thousand Jocks up the jungle suffering from screaming ab-dabs and going mad for women, beer and haggis'. In his usual way, Bamforth tries to evade the responsibility for the insult by ending his little speech with a joke. But Macleish will not be pacified by a joke.

This time the squabble becomes a full-blown argument with Macleish leaving his post on guard at the window and asking Evans to take his place so that he can deal with Bamforth. It seems clear that they are both spoiling for a fight and Smith can see that Bamforth is purposely aggravating Macleish. He knows they are behaving like children: 'For God's sake grow up, the pair of you!'

This is the second time in the play that Bamforth has been involved in fights with one of the other soldiers, the first time playfully with Evans and this time more seriously with Macleish. If you were Macleish, would you be offended by Bamforth's insults? How would you behave? Do you think Smith was right when he said that Bamforth is taunting Macleish in order to get Macleish into trouble? Should Smith have interfered?

In the middle of this Mitchem and Johnstone return, only to find a full-blown fight going on and no one, apparently, guarding the windows. Mitchem deals with the situation by falling back on army discipline, ordering all the men to line up as if for inspection. His anger explodes: 'Shower! Useless shower! That's all you are. The lot of you. I could have been a regiment of ruddy Nips and I walked through that door.'

It is, of course, the responsibility of Lance-Corporal Macleish and he has to apologize and also try to explain. Macleish, however, does not reveal that it was Bamforth he was fighting and squabbling with. 'I forget now,' he says. Mitchem threatens to punish everyone until the culprit owns up and then Bamforth does so.

Stop for a moment and consider this. Why does Macleish refuse to blame Bamforth? Why does Bamforth then own up? In simple army terms Bamforth has insulted a senior officer. Is this a matter of 'insubordination' as the army would call it, or does Macleish see the quarrel as a private matter? What would you have done if you were Macleish?

After Bamforth has owned up it is now Mitchem's job to reprimand him, which he does at some length using language which is unofficial but which both of them – and all the other soldiers – well understand: 'Don't try and come that hard-case stuff with me, son' and, 'You're a non-runner, son, I start favourite halfway down the course before the off. You haven't got a chance.'

Notice that Johnstone calls Bamforth 'lad', and Mitchem calls him 'lad' and 'son'. Why should they do this do you think? Does it tell you anything about their relationship?

Mitchem does not allow Bamforth to say anything by way of explanation or in his own defence but merely tells him how he should behave. As soon as he has done this he addresses the whole patrol, putting them in the picture about their situation. He puts them at their ease by being absolutely matter-of-fact and he gives them hope by explaining exactly how they will organize the journey back to base-camp. Mitchem's training and character are clearly illustrated here. He defuses a tense situation in a sensible and calm way.

Macleish's worries are illustrated here when his questions to Mitchem about other British forces up-country reveal his concern about his younger brother. The audience is also kept informed about the movements of the army so that we can form a larger picture of the background of the play. We see the soldiers on patrol as part of a much larger army.

Mitchem also reorganizes the men. Bamforth and Evans are given guard-duty at the windows and Whitaker is asked about communication on the radio. Against Johnstone's criticism: 'How much a week do they pay you for this, lad?' Mitchem immediately defends Whitaker: 'It's not his fault. The battery's dis.' Mitchem and Johnstone discuss the radio-message and the difference in their personalities is clearly shown, Johnstone becoming very angry over being given a useless battery by HQ and Mitchem saying, 'We'll sort that out when we get back,' and 'It's no good flapping over that.'

Notice that when left to themselves Johnstone and Mitchem talk together. Is this because they are the two senior soldiers on the patrol or because they have anything else in common? Would they be friends in a different situation?

The next important and frightening episode in the play is Whitaker's successful attempt to raise something on the radio-transmitter. Instead of base-camp coming through, the patrol hears the voice of a Japanese radio-operator. The stage-directions tell us that the patrol 'reacts with forced humour', making jokes about 'rice for tea' and 'Bring on the geisha girls.' The only two who realize the full implications are Whitaker and Mitchem. When Whitaker explains that the range of the radio-receiver might be under ten miles, they all gradually begin to realize that the Japanese forces must have broken through the British lines further up-country and are now making their way south. Macleish becomes almost panic-stricken about the fate of his younger brother who had been sent up-country.

Again Mitchem takes control and makes practical preparations for dealing with a Japanese attack. He tells the patrol that they are letting their imaginations run riot and that the evidence of one Japanese voice on the radio-set is not conclusive.

Read again Mitchem's words from the bottom of page 31, beginning: 'Now just shut up. Listen,' as far as the bottom of page 32. Try to follow his train of thought. In what ways does he try to comfort the men in his patrol and restore their confidence? Why, do you think, does he decide to return to base-camp as quickly as possible? What would you have done?

One crisis follows another here, for as soon as Mitchem has organized the preparations for the return, Bamforth, who is on sentry-duty, sees a man moving outside. There is a degree of tension while the others try to locate him and before he is identified as a Japanese soldier. The man seems to have slipped away to smoke a cigarette and, unfortunately, discovers the track leading up to the hut.

All would have been well; the Japanese soldier might not have entered the hut had not Whitaker in his worry forgotten to move the radio-receiver from the table where it is in clear view from the window. Mitchem's order had been, 'Let's have you over by the wall! And bring your gear,' but Whitaker had remembered to hide only himself and not his transmitter. When told by Mitchem to fetch it, the stage-direction tells us that 'Whitaker moves as if to cross to table, but changes his mind and hugs the wall in terror.' The Japanese soldier, seeing the radio, opens the door of the hut, presumably to investigate and is immediately grabbed by Johnstone so that he cannot move or shout. Mitchem dashes to the door, covering the jungle with the sten-gun, while Johnstone appeals to the other members of the patrol who have been crouching, hiding below the windows.

Put yourself in the place of the Japanese soldier. Why have you left your patrol? Why did you follow the track up to the hut and why did you, alone, enter the hut when you saw the radio-transmitter?

Evans, who is on guard-duty with Bamforth and has a loaded rifle, does not have enough courage to kill the Japanese prisoner. His first inclination was to use his rifle but the bullet would have killed Johnstone too. When Johnstone shouts, telling him to kill the man with his bayonet, Evans' nerve breaks. Macleish will not stab the man either. It is left to Bamforth who seems perfectly prepared to do so, saying, 'It's only the same as carving up a pig.'

Mitchem's return saves the prisoner's life because he wants to keep the Japanese alive. He communicates with the prisoner in pidgin English, telling him to keep quiet and that he will not be hurt. The audience would find it quite amusing that the sergeant speaks very slowly and patiently in English to the Japanese prisoner. In fact the prisoner understands mime rather than the broken English. Bamforth cannot resist the temptation to tease the Japanese with the bayonet. The playwright has released the tension by amusing the audience after the shock of a few minutes before. The tension is further lessened by the rather pathetic sight of the prisoner divested of his armaments, which are described in the stage-directions as a revolver, a string of hand grenades and a long two-edged bayonet.

Johnstone teases the other members of the patrol now that they are no longer frightened of the Japanese prisoner. Macleish tries to defend himself and the others by asserting that they could not kill the prisoner when Johnstone asked for help because it is against the code of the Geneva Convention. 'You cannot order men to put a bayonet in an unarmed prisoner.'

Mitchem quickly restores order by placing Evans and Whitaker at the windows and giving Bamforth control over the prisoner. It is worth noticing that Mitchem offers the sten-gun to Bamforth in order to guard the prisoner but Bamforth refuses, picking up the Japanese bayonet and saying, 'I'll settle for this.' Why do you think he does this? Remember that at the end of the play, in a very similar situation, Mitchem offers the sten to Whitaker, who takes it, and in panic shoots the prisoner. Do you think Bamforth would have reacted in the same way?

Certainly Bamforth seems to show no fear of the prisoner, treating him rather like a performing animal which can be taught tricks. Neither is his language very complimentary, calling the Japanese prisoner 'Shortarse' and 'you asiatic get'. The stage-directions tell us that Bamforth is 'delighted' when the prisoner understands that he has to put his hands on his head or up towards the ceiling. The playwright adds a touch of humour by making Bamforth speak in what is the popular conception of English spoken by the Japanese — changing the letter 'r' to 'l' and adding the 'l' to other words, as in 'Flingers up on blonce'. The audience will probably smile at this foolishness and yet at the same time feel sorry that the prisoner is being exploited. However, it all seems rather harmless fun. What are your feelings about this episode? Do you think Bamforth's behaviour is acceptable?

The problem of what to do with the prisoner occupies the minds of Mitchem and Johnstone. Mitchem's first thought is to take the prisoner back to camp with them, alive, whereas Johnstone's first thought is clearly that the prisoner should be killed, showing his doubt of the wisdom of Mitchem's plan by admitting 'You're in charge.' Mitchem does not debate further with Johnstone but says curtly 'That's right.'

The arrival of one Japanese soldier at the hut may well mean that there are many others nearby so Mitchem organizes a further reconnaissance patrol consisting of Macleish and Smith. Macleish uses the euphemism 'Supposing we should . . . make contact?' to ask what they should do if they see any Japanese. Mitchem, cautious as ever, says, 'Don't. Not if you can help it.' When the reader or the audience already knows the end of the play, there is irony in Evans's remark about the area outside the hut: 'Quiet. Quiet as a grave.' It does become a grave for six men before much longer. Do you think the playwright means us to take this as a hint, a clue, about the possible ending of the play, or is it just the sort of cliché that any man would use in Evans's position?

While Evans and Macleish are away, Mitchem once more tries to communicate with the prisoner, again by speaking slowly and carefully. Bamforth again makes the prisoner raise and lower his hands.

The impossibility of communicating with the prisoner depresses Mitchem: 'What's the use . . .' and again Johnstone is quick to repeat his belief that 'We should have done him first time off.'

Again Johnstone tries to persuade Mitchem that the wisest course of action is to kill the Japanese prisoner. What is your opinion about this? Do you think Johnstone is right? Do you think Johnstone wants to kill the prisoner for the reasons he gives or has he some other motive?

Johnstone is sarcastic about Mitchem's worrying over the prospect of writing a report 'Because we do a Jap'. He clearly thinks of the prisoner as less than human. His logic is clear: 'We whip him out and knock him off, that's all. We can't take prisoners. We're out to do a job.' Unlike Mitchem, Johnstone is thinking of short-term solutions. Mitchem, on the other hand, can see that the prisoner might well be very useful as a source of information for the British back at basecamp: 'Because if anybody knows the strength of Nips behind our lines it's him.'

This train of thought leads Mitchem to reveal what he is thinking about their situation – not to the rest of the patrol, only to Johnstone. 'So far on this outing out it's been the biggest muck-up in the history of the British Army, and that's saying a lot. We've wandered round, the set's packed in, we've no idea what's going on and if ever there was an organized shambles – my God, this is it.' The discussion between Mitchem and Johnstone (about the prisoner's life) is finally cut short by Mitchem's assertion, 'I'll put the bayonet in his guts myself.' And then Mitchem changes the subject.

This rather gruelling and serious subject is immediately contrasted with the next episode in the play in which the prisoner shows Bamforth photographs of his wife and family. Because the prisoner doesn't speak, we have to learn about his family through Bamforth, with all the amusement that that entails. Bamforth's long speech on page 45 talking about the photographs is a mixture of amused interest and rudeness. He does, after all, call the prisoner 'you stupid raving imbecile'. Through Bamforth we learn that the prisoner has a wife, 'very nice' even though 'a bit short in the pins', two children and a new baby. Encouraged by this act of friendliness on the part of the prisoner, Bamforth once more gets him to raise and lower his hands. Why do you think the playwright includes this information about the Japanese prisoner's family life? Does it make you, the audience, regard the prisoner differently? How does it make you feel about him?

After this rapport between Bamforth and the prisoner, Johnstone again shows his contempt: 'We should have done him in when he first turned up,' and then after Bamforth has given the prisoner a cigarette Johnstone knocks it out of his mouth. Bamforth and Johnstone fight each other, Bamforth knocking Johnstone on to the floor. Mitchem's first shout to stop the scuffle is 'Corporal Johnstone!' indicating that he thinks that Johnstone started it. Under army regulations, a private soldier who assaults an NCO is put on a charge and this clearly is what Johnstone hopes will happen. 'You've done it this time, Bamforth! You've shot your load. As sure as God, you'll get three years for that.' Mitchem reinforces this: 'You're on a charge, Bamforth. You're under open arrest.'

However, just at this moment Bamforth is saved by the lookout, Evans, spotting someone coming up the track towards the hut. This turns out to be Macleish and Smith returning from their reconnaissance mission. The arrest and charge against Bamforth goes no further for the moment.

If you were Bamforth, how would you have defended yourself against a charge of striking a superior? You could act out this scene with a group of you, imagining it as a court. Would Bamforth have been given a sentence of three years, do you think, after his evidence had been heard? Apart from army regulations, do you think he was justified in fighting with Johnstone? What do you think was his real reason for doing so?

The return of Macleish and Smith brings another piece of unwelcome news for the patrol which is only what we in the audience have already suspected. The Japanese army has broken through the British lines in strength and is pouring down-country towards Singapore. Macleish and Smith have covered the entrance to the trail with branches but it is clear that they are now in a very dangerous position. Mitchem immediately sees the problem: 'It's put the kybosh on the journey back. We can't move out of here just yet, and that's a certainty.' He thinks quickly, works out how long it will take for the Japanese to reach the British base-camp, and then calculates that if his patrol travel quickly they can reach the base-camp before the Japanese.

Again Johnstone's reaction is merely negative: 'We haven't got a chance.' He is especially sure that there is no chance of getting home safely with the prisoner 'in tow'. This time Mitchem agrees, saying, 'We're ditching him.'

The other thought in Mitchem's mind is the hope of contacting the base by radio and this he urges Whitaker to do. Whitaker knows that it is dangerous to try to do so. 'If there are any Japs near here switched to receive they'll get a fix on us.' Mitchem realizes this too but believes 'That can't be helped.' The patrol and the audience listen to the crackly reception on the radio, fearing the worst and hoping for contact with base-camp. Their fears are realized; not only is there a Japanese radio-announcer speaking but he is speaking to this patrol, with the threatening message: 'We – you – come – to – get.' While the horror of this is sinking in, the patrol turn to look at the Japanese prisoner; he misinterprets their interest and thinks he should show them the tricks he has learnt. The curtain falls for the interval.

During the interval what do you think would be the main topic of conversation among the audience? What are your feelings about the play at this point? Are you depressed, hopeful, amused, or what? Give your reasons. If you did not already know the story, what would you guess was going to happen next and how would you think the play would end?

When you look back at Act One you will see that it consists of a series of episodes or 'happenings'. Write these episodes out for yourself in a list and against each one write an adjective which describes what is going on, such as 'amusing', 'frightening' and so on. Now look at your whole list for Act One and note how the playwright has contrasted the atmosphere and purpose of different episodes. How has he built up the tension in the play? Would you have altered the structure at all? If so, how and why?

ACT TWO

When this Act opens, we learn from our programmes that it is thirty minutes later – about the same time as the interval. The impression of reality is continued in this way. The patrol is in exactly the same frightening situation as they were at the end of Act One except that the time-lapse has allowed the truth about their predicament to sink in and for them to get used to the idea.

The stage-directions tell us that when a bird sings out in the jungle, Whitaker raises his rifle and then 'glances round the room in embarrassment'. He is clearly jumpy and nervous, and repeatedly asks Mitchem the time. The scene begins with a story told by Whitaker to Smith who are both still on guard-duty. It is the first time in the play that we have heard Whitaker talking freely in this way, even though the story about having a watch stolen seems quite unimportant. However, it does tell a little more about Whitaker and the things he values, and that he intended the watch as a present for his father.

Why, do you think, does the playwright begin Act Two in this way? Is this what you would have done? Why does Whitaker keep talking? (Eventually the stage-directions tell us but do you think the audience would guess the reason?)

Mitchem offers his water-bottle to the Japanese prisoner 'who accepts it gratefully'. Is this kindness on Mitchem's part or something else?

Then begins the long conversation between Mitchem and Macleish about the fate of the prisoner which lasts for ten pages of the text. Clearly, the underlying worry in Macleish's mind is the fate of his younger brother, Donald, who is with the British contingent up-country. If the Japanese army has broken through, what, Macleish wonders, has happened to these British soldiers? It is clearly in his mind that his brother might be a prisoner in the hands of the Japanese and, because he needs to think that his brother will be well-treated, he needs to think that the Japanese are decent, saying, 'He doesn't seem a bad sort of bloke.'

It was Macleish who had been out on the reconnaissance patrol with Smith and had seen for himself the Japanese army pouring down the main track. His worry is about the speed with which the Japanese have, apparently, defeated the British forward troops and that his brother is possibly captured. 'You hear all kinds of things. As if they're almost . . . animals. But this bloke seems a decent sort of bloke.' It seems important to Macleish that the Japanese prisoner is 'a family man himself'.

Mitchem does not help him by agreeing, saying, 'You put a bloke in uniform and push him overseas and he's a different bloke to what he was before.' Why do you think he says this? Why does he not allow Macleish to believe that his brother will be well-treated? Is Mitchem being hard-hearted, thoughtless, realistic, or what? What would you have said in his situation?

In fact, the playwright gives us the opportunity to understand Mitchem a little here because, in spite of having to play the competent sergeant, he is clearly as disillusioned as Bamforth, describing the Japanese as 'nigs like us who don't know why we're here or what it's all in aid of'.

The next problem that Macleish discusses is one with which the audience might easily sympathize – whether he is able to kill a man. He feels that he needs to explain, or even apologize for, the fact that he did not and could not bayonet the Japanese soldier when Johnstone first captured him. It was too intimate and personal. He explains that he could kill if the target is 'something you can put a bullet in and not have to . . . have to look into its eyes'. Notice that Macleish talks about the enemy here as 'it' just as Johnstone does in his squabble with Bamforth at the end of the play. Perhaps depersonalizing the enemy makes the conscience clearer about having to kill one of them. Macleish still sees fighting in a war as a game with a code of chivalry, rather like medieval knights and jousting. He could kill someone outside, he says, because, 'Outside he's got a fighting chance.'

What do you think of Macleish's reasoning? Has he got a good point or do you think he is just apologizing for cowardice? Do you think it is possible to predict whether you would or would not kill in an extreme situation? Can you think of any situations where you would? Mitchem says that Macleish's problem is that he thinks too much. Do you agree?

We learn more about Mitchem from his next speech which is an outburst of criticism of women. Women, he says, are at the root of most of the troubles in the world. In particular, they flatter a man until he joins the army and wears a uniform. The result is that a 'Few weeks after that he's on his back with his feet in the air and a hole as big as a fist in his belly. And he's nothing.' When the soldier is dead, 'Do you think that bint is going to float off to a nunnery?' What does this outburst tell us about Mitchem? He seems fairly specific. Do you think he is telling a true story, perhaps his own? Is his home life unhappy? Why does he tell all this to Macleish?

Mitchem brings the discussion back to the prisoner and very patiently tries to explain to Macleish that he will have to kill the prisoner rather than take him with them back to camp. Macleish seems very slow to understand this, either because he *is* very slow or, more probably, because he will not accept the fact that a prisoner can be killed in cold blood. He is almost certainly thinking of his brother, who may be in Japanese hands, and cannot face the thought that he too could be killed. Mitchem seems reluctant to tell Macleish straight out of his intention, but allows the questioning to go on and on. This becomes almost unbearable for the audience who have realized Mitchem's intention long before Macleish does so. Do you think this is kindness and patience on the part of Mitchem or do you interpret his reluctance differently? Put yourself in the place of Mitchem. How would you have explained your intention to Macleish?

When Macleish finally does realize the truth, he protests repeatedly, saying, 'You're not going to knock him off?' He repeats that the Japanese soldier is a prisoner of war who gave himself up. Is this true? Did the Japanese give himself up or is Macleish muddling this with something else? Can you explain his thinking?

As if the question and answer session about the fate of the Japanese prisoner had not been searing enough, the next exchange concerns exactly how it is to be achieved. The audience realizes that Mitchem will have to kill the prisoner quietly and quickly and that all Macleish's protestations are pointless. Mitchem knows it is an awful thing to do: 'It stinks to me to do for him.' At the same time Macleish is interpreting it personally: 'I've got a brother who could just be sitting back – right now. Like him.'

The argument about the fate of the prisoner becomes almost a personal squabble between Mitchem and Macleish. However, we can soon see that it is a very unequal argument. Look again at pages 60 and 61 and try to read it as a bitter argument. It is clear that Mitchem has all the reasons and that Macleish can only think of personal insults. He says of Mitchem, 'You're off your nut,' 'You're talking out the back of your head' and 'You're talking through your hat.' Mitchem says to Macleish, 'You're as bad as Bamforth, boy.' Do you think he is? Can you write out a list of the various arguments put forward by Mitchem to try to defeat Macleish's objections? At the side of each argument say whether you think it is true or false.

Does this exchange between the two men tell us anything new about them or do they continue to behave in exactly the way you had expected? By which of the two standpoints are you more convinced? Which of the two men do you admire most? Why?

The discussion is brought to a close by Whitaker yet again asking the time. From argument, the play changes to action with several things happening in quick succession: the prisoner indicates that he wants one of his own cigarettes and gives one to Macleish; Mitchem wakes up Bamforth, Evans and Johnstone and there is humorous banter about Bamforth's dream. Bamforth wants to go outside and makes a joke of that too: 'So what am I supposed to do? Write out an application?'

While Bamforth is out of the hut, two misunderstandings arise amongst the rest of the patrol. Firstly, Johnstone and Mitchem discuss the fate of the prisoner now that 'It's settled what we're going to do with him.' Johnstone's first thought is who will do the job, and when asked by Mitchem if he is volunteering says, 'I don't mind.' Johnstone reminds Mitchem that the prisoner must be killed quickly and 'wants a professional touch'. It is clear from his attitude that Johnstone is thinking of himself or Mitchem. Does this conversation with Mitchem tell you anything about Johnstone? Which adjectives would you use to describe his character? Do you think he is a good soldier?

The next incident concerns the Japanese prisoner and the cigarette which he has given to Macleish. It is Johnstone who initiates this investigation by declaring, 'I wouldn't touch his stinking wog tobacco,' and bringing Macleish's reply, 'It's just an ordinary cigarette.' Anger flares when the members of the patrol discover that the prisoner has a packet of British army-issue cigarettes. Mitchem immediately jumps to the conclusion that the prisoner 'must have thieved them from the lads up-country'.

Look again at the reaction, on pages 66 and 67, of the British soldiers to the suspicion that the prisoner has been looting cigarettes from captured British soldiers. We already know about Johnstone's character and his feelings towards the prisoner. We have also witnessed Macleish's anxiety about his brother being a prisoner of the Japanese. But we are hardly prepared for the ferocity of Evans's reaction. He says, 'There's some of them would kill their mothers for a drag,' and 'He wants a lesson, Sarge. He ought to have a lesson taught to him.' Did you expect such a reaction from Evans?

Mitchem wonders what other 'loot' the prisoner is carrying and asks Macleish to go through the prisoner's pockets. Johnstone again shows the spiteful side of his nature by slowly and carefully tearing up the photographs of the prisoner's family, and then, when the prisoner reacts to this, Macleish 'strikes him across the face'.

It is this incident which greets Bamforth when he re-enters the hut. He is astounded and disgusted by the way in which the rest of the patrol is treating the prisoner and embarrasses all of them by revealing that it was he who had given the prisoner the British cigarettes.

Look at Macleish's speech on page 69, the one in which he is 'searching for words'. Why does he find his emotions so hard to describe? Why do you think he finds it necessary to explain to Bamforth why he behaved as he did? What is Bamforth's reaction to Macleish's explanation? What adjectives would you use to describe Bamforth's tone towards Macleish and the others?

Bamforth pinions the prisoner's arms and holds him so that Macleish can hit him and at this point Mitchem intervenes. 'OK, Bamforth, jack it in.' Why does he intervene? Has Bamforth gone too far? Do you think Bamforth is justified in his anger? Try to explain his sarcasm.

Evans tries to make up for the way they have treated the prisoner by finding and returning the torn fragments of photographs. Look again at how he does this on pages 70–71. How is he feeling about what has happened? Is this a new side to Evans's character or is it what you would have expected of him? How do you think you would feel in his position if you discovered that you had been cruel to someone by mistake?

It is Johnstone who pursues the matter further by inspecting the Japanese prisoner's cigarette-case and discovering that it was made in Birmingham. The playwright once again swings our feelings against the prisoner because even Bamforth cannot find an explanation for this. He may have given the prisoner British cigarettes but he certainly has not given him a cigarette-case. Immediately both Mitchem and Evans are again suspicious, Evans believing that the prisoner has been 'Half-inching from the boys up country.' Macleish thinks the same. 'It's pretty obvious he's pinched the thing.'

Bamforth again tries to protect the prisoner by trying to find a convincing explanation for his possession of a British cigarette-case. He uses the example of his little sister back in England who has a doll which was made in Japan. He tries to make fun of their accusations by telling the story that his little sister had killed Japanese children in order to steal the doll. Mitchem points out that the Japanese export knick-knacks; they don't buy them from Britain. Bamforth does not press his explanation; perhaps he knows it is not terribly convincing.

Bamforth's next ploy is to turn from defence to attack by revealing that the Japanese soldier is not alone in collecting souvenirs of the enemy; Whitaker has 'the biggest hoard of loot in the Far East, bar none'. Why does he do this, do you think? If you look at pages 74 and 75 Bamforth tells them about all the 'Jap swag' collected by Whitaker, which Whitaker tries to deny and play down. Is Whitaker embarrassed by Bamforth's revelation, or ashamed, or what? How would you have felt in his situation? Would you have expected this of Whitaker from what you already know of him?

This time it is Smith who tries to defend Whitaker against Bamforth's accusations by repeating, 'Leave the kid alone, Bammo. There's no harm in it,' 'Let him alone, Bamforth,' and 'Can't you leave the lad alone.' Do you agree with Smith that Bamforth is going too far? Is there anything wrong, in your opinion, with collecting souvenirs of war? Why, do you think, has Whitaker collected them?

Bamforth shows his disgust for Whitaker's weak personality by calling him, 'Whining Whitaker! The boy who has a nervous breakdown at the thought of Madame Butterfly.' After Whitaker's admission of having collected all his war souvenirs as swops, Bamforth invites Macleish to compare Whitaker's hoard with that of the Japanese prisoner. 'Now, go on, Jock, beat up the Nip.'

Macleish's reply is typical of the semi-official language which he uses. 'You still haven't proved, to my satisfaction, that that's the way he got the case.' Can you find any other example in the play of this distinctive mode of speech of Macleish's? Does this tell you anything about him? Macleish's next remark, 'Och, what's it matter anyway . . .' finishes the discussion of that topic and the playwright prepares the audience for the next.

Whitaker and Smith have been on guard-duty and Whitaker has constantly asked the time. He does so again and this time Mitchem changes the guard so that Macleish and Evans take their turn. This move releases Whitaker and in the next few minutes the audience hears more about Whitaker's life back at home. He asks to borrow Evans's magazine which gives Bamforth yet another opportunity to tease him. 'They lock their daughters up in Newcastle when he's on leave. Go on, Whitaker, you've never been with a bint in your life.'

When Whitaker starts to talk about his girlfriend, Mary, it is the more kindly Smith who takes over the questioning. Why does the playwright do this, do you think? Look at the questions which Smith puts to Whitaker on pages 79 and 80. How would you describe Smith's attitude from these questions?

The audience will find Whitaker's description of his girl and the way they passed their time quite touching and sad. Why is this? After all, Bamforth has tried all through the play to show how foolish and inadequate Whitaker is. Look again at Whitaker's two long speeches on page 79. How do these make you feel about him? Do you think it is a good description of first love?

The romantic atmosphere is helped by the playwright's next stage-direction: 'It is early evening and the light has begun to dim. The jungle is silent and a stillness falls upon the patrol. Bamforth begins to sing – quietly and with a touch of sadness.' It is ironic that the song he chooses is about a handsome young private dying. What effect do you think this song would have on the audience? If you did not know the end of the play, would you guess at this point that their deaths are inevitable? Give your reasons.

This quiet interlude precedes the last, dramatic episode of the play. The audience will already be familiar with Bamforth's caring for the prisoner and sharing his water-bottle with him. When Johnstone, supported by Mitchem, refuses to allow Bamforth to give the prisoner a drink, Bamforth is incredulous. However, the audience knows something which Bamforth does not, having witnessed the long discussion between Mitchem and Macleish. Mitchem has decided to kill the Japanese prisoner rather than take him with them. Therefore, logically, there is no need to waste precious drinking-water on a man who is about to die. Do you agree with this attitude or would you have given water to the prisoner? Give your reasons.

Incidentally, a situation in which the audience knows something which the characters in a play do not, is called 'dramatic irony'. In this case Bamforth is ignorant of the proposed fate of the prisoner, and reacts with horror when he suspects it. Why do you think the playwright uses this device?

Johnstone sums up what is to become of the prisoner, 'It's cobbler's for him.' Both Mitchem and Johnstone refer to the prisoner as 'it' instead of 'he' which contrasts with Bamforth's assertion that 'He's a man.' What does this contrast tell us about all three men?

It seems inevitable that Bamforth will try to defend the prisoner against Mitchem and Johnstone, but what the audience cannot be sure of is the reaction of all the other members of the patrol, especially remembering Macleish's objections earlier in Act Two. In fact, Bamforth appeals to each of the others, one by one, to help him and when each of them refuses, he registers his disgust. To Whitaker he says, 'You're a gutless slob!' to Smith, 'The plodding on has stopped. Right here. Right here you stop and make a stand,' and to Macleish,

'I hope they carve your brother up. Get that? I hope they carve your bloody brother up!'

What is your reaction? What would you have done had you been one of the patrol? Would you have sided with Bamforth or Mitchem? Give your reasons. Would you have let emotion or common sense rule your decision?

Mitchem orders Whitaker to 'Grab a gun and cover the Nip' while he and Johnstone try to overpower Bamforth. Do you think Mitchem chose the right man or should one of the others have had the sten-gun? Was Mitchem's order to Whitaker a considered one or a hasty idea? As it turns out, Whitaker's fear and nervousness accelerates the death of all of them because his shooting of the prisoner alerts all the Japanese in the neighbourhood.

Look at page 84 again, at the different reactions of Mitchem and Whitaker to the prisoner's death: 'Whitaker drops the sten and buries his face in his hands,' while Mitchem says, 'Well, that should roust out every Nip from here to Tokyo. You've made a mess of that, lad.' How would you explain their different reactions?

Bamforth's sarcastic remark to Whitaker is cut short as Mitchem 'strikes him across the face'. All of them now realize the extreme danger of their situation and Mitchem immediately orders their exit from the hut. He speaks in short, terse sentences, showing the sense of urgency now. His last thought before they leave is to try once more to contact base to warn them of the Japanese advance because he knows, 'We haven't got a snowball's chance in Hell of getting back.' Johnstone gets no response but leaves the set switched on.

After the members of the patrol have left the hut one by one, the radio-set comes to life and the audience can hear the voice of the British radio-operator back at base-camp. It is ironic that the patrol has missed this by only a few seconds.

The patrol has now left the stage and the events of the next few seconds are conveyed to the audience by sound-effects. They 'hear the sound of one or two rifles and the screams of dying men'. Johnstone comes back into the hut, wounded, and off-stage we hear Whitaker crying 'God! . . . God! . . . Mother! . . .'

Johnstone's reaction to the British Army radio-operator is, 'Get knotted! All of you! You hear? The whole damn lot of you!' Do you think this is sarcasm or desperation or what?

The play finishes with Johnstone smoking one of the dead prisoner's cigarettes and using the prisoner's white scarf as a signal that he would like to surrender. Imagine you are Johnstone. What thoughts run through your head as you lie in the hut waiting for the Japanese patrol to enter?

What do you think your feelings would be as the stage-lights fade and the audience begins to clap at the end of the play? All the actors will come to the front of the stage and take a bow. Do you think this is appropriate or do you think the play should just end, as it does on television or on film? If you were directing, how would you organize the end of the play?

Characters

MITCHEM

Mitchem is the sergeant in charge of this reconnaissance patrol. He has been sent out with six men from base-camp presumably to establish the whereabouts and strength of the Japanese army. He establishes five of his men in a deserted mining-hut and then with his second-in-command, Johnstone, leaves them for a further sortie to establish that they are in a safe place for a rest before they travel back. He is clearly an experienced and competent soldier.

Because Mitchem is the senior man on the patrol he cannot seem too friendly with any of the others. His authority must be seen to be fair and equitable. His natural companion would seem to be his second-in-command, Johnstone, although he seems to have very little in common with him. As the senior NCO in charge of a reconnaissance patrol, he does his job thoroughly and professionally as is demonstrated on his return when he discovers Macleish and Bamforth about to fight. He restores order quickly, gives Bamforth a thorough telling-off and then outlines their position and his plans for the future.

There are several crises while the patrol is in the hut. There is the shock of hearing the Japanese voice on the radio-transmitter, the capture of the Japanese prisoner, the taunting message from the Japanese radio-operator and lastly the panic which results in the prisoner being killed. Throughout all of these, Mitchem keeps calm and is a good example to his men. He does not panic but thinks quickly, assesses the situation and then plans ahead. He has a tremendous responsibility – the lives of seven men – and always behaves professionally.

Whitaker's constant questioning of Mitchem about the time taxes his patience but he copes with it and, in fact, defends Whitaker against Johnstone. He knows Whitaker is young and incompetent and says, 'It's not his fault. The battery's dis. OK, Sammy. Have another go. Better give it one more try.' Later in the play he shows great patience with Macleish who cannot, or will not, understand that the Japanese prisoner will have to be killed to ensure the safety of the rest of them. Perhaps he recognizes in Macleish's doubts some of his own. The playwright allows nearly ten pages of dialogue between Macleish and Mitchem arguing about the fate of the prisoner. This allows the audience to follow the debate too and to decide for themselves who is right.

Bamforth is a continual trial to Mitchem because he constantly barracks both the corporal and the lance-corporal, trying to undermine their authority. But Mitchem recognizes the truth about Bamforth and after telling him off gives him no right of reply. He knows that Bamforth has a clever way with words and is devious. However, Mitchem seems unprepared for Bamforth's spirited defence of the Japanese prisoner at the end of the play. In handing the sten-gun to the nervy Whitaker, he is almost signing the death-warrant for all of them. Although this act seems foolish in real life, it is necessary dramatically.

In general, Mitchem keeps his distance from any personal bickering in the patrol and we learn nothing about his private life in the way we learn about Evans, Smith and Whitaker. However, during the long conversation with Macleish, Mitchem does make an impassioned attack on women, saying that they are the cause of war. 'Half the scrapping in this world is over judies.' His philosophy is pragmatic: 'I'm not a thinking kind of man,' he says, 'I look at facts.' This tirade may tell us something about Mitchem's private life and his bitterness about war. He makes it clear that, unlike Johnstone, he does not intend to kill the prisoner from malice, but that after having considered all the possibilities, that is the only choice left to him.

Looking at the end of the play, whose fault do you think it was that the situation got out of hand? Can Mitchem be criticized for his handling of any of the crises?

If you were one of the patrol, what would your opinion be of Mitchem's leadership? Which qualities in him do you admire and which do you dislike? Would you be happy to go out with him on another reconnaissance mission? Imagine that you are Whitaker or

Evans with a girlfriend at home. What would you tell her about Mitchem when she asked?

JOHNSTONE

Johnstone is a corporal and second-in-command to Mitchem. He is the least likeable of all the characters in the play because he does not seem to have one redeeming virtue except, perhaps, that he is good at his job of fighting. Although he is a corporal, he makes little contribution to the running of the patrol and, unlike Mitchem, undermines the men's confidence by sarcasm. This makes him a bad disciplinarian, especially in comparison with Mitchem.

When we first meet Johnstone, he immediately squabbles with Bamforth, over whom he continually 'pulls rank'. He calls Bamforth 'lad' when there cannot be much difference in their ages and is clearly patronizing and domineering. Evans remarks to Bamforth that 'Johnno's got it in for you' and, because of this, the audience warms to Bamforth and his opposition to Johnstone.

But we learn most about Johnstone from his attitude towards the Japanese prisoner. He it is who captures the Japanese in a professional and practised manner and then demands that one of the others bayonet the prisoner. The playwright gives us all the details: 'Not that way, lad! You'll only bust a bone. Feel for it first, then ram it in.' The audience finds this horrific as do the other soldiers in the patrol and sympathizes with Macleish when Johnstone accuses his comrades of cowardice.

JOHNSTONE: A right lot I've got landed with! Not one of you had the guts to give me a hand.
MACLEISH: You weren't in need of help. You cannot order men to put a bayonet in an unarmed prisoner.

It is Johnstone who continually shows cruelty to the Japanese prisoner. After the episode of the cigarettes and the cigarette-case, the stage-directions tell us that 'Johnstone, slowly and carefully, tears the photographs into pieces and drops these and the wallet on the floor.' When

Bamforth offers the prisoner a drink of water, Johnstone prevents him, saying, 'There's no more buckshees for the Nippo, Bamforth.' The whole question of the fate of the prisoner which had been so carefully discussed by Macleish and Mitchem is revealed starkly by Johnstone: 'It's cobbler's for him.' In fact, the audience clearly gets the impression that Johnstone would enjoy killing the prisoner, having earlier volunteered to do so. And finally, in the last squabble of all, Johnstone shows his ruthlessness and lack of humanity towards the prisoner when he describes him as 'it' and 'a bloody Nip'.

The dramatic end to the play with all the men killed except Johnstone leaves the audience wondering whether he will be treated in the same way by his Japanese captors as he would have treated his prisoner. The introductory notes to the play tell us the author's purpose in choosing Johnstone as the soldier who surrenders. 'This should not be accepted as any sign of cowardice. He is, in fact, a soldier who has done all that he can in his fight against the enemy and now, as a wounded man, is surrendering and therefore making himself a liability to the enemy – will no doubt later attempt to escape – rather than allow himself to be killed uselessly.'

Write down five adjectives which you would use to praise Johnstone if you were, for example, recommending him for promotion; then write down five adjectives which you think accurately describe him from the point of view of the other men in the patrol.

Do you think Johnstone would make a good sergeant? How would he have behaved if Mitchem had been killed and he, Johnstone, had had to make the decisions about the Japanese prisoner and the return to base-camp?

What qualities in him have persuaded his superiors that he should hold the rank of corporal? What do you think he might do as a job in civilian life? Do you like him or dislike him? Why?

MACLEISH

At first sight it seems that Macleish is a stereotyped Scotsman who is touchy about being teased and quite humourless. But he soon reveals a kindliness and regard for others which persuades us to like him. He is clearly devoted to his younger brother, having tried to organize a transfer to his own unit, presumably so that he can look after him. Macleish's first thought when he understands the implications of the Japanese voice on the radio-transmitter is for the welfare of his younger brother. Mitchem has to tell him four times to shut up.

Macleish takes his position as a newly created lance-corporal very seriously and his speech-patterns reflect his reading of army regulations: 'It so happens that I accepted the rank of lance-corporal. Having accepted the rank, and the responsibility that goes with it, I feel it's my duty to back up my fellow NCOs. And that decision is regardless of any personal prejudices I might hold.' He sounds pompous and as a result is mercilessly teased by Bamforth. In fact he takes his position so seriously that being taunted by Bamforth is too much for his temper. The others can see that Macleish is being pushed by Bamforth. 'You dim Scotch crone!' says Smith, 'It's what he wants! He's dying for you to put him one on.' Macleish is even prepared to lose his rank as lance-corporal in order to teach Bamforth a lesson. However, when the imminent fight between them is interrupted by the entrance of Johnstone and Mitchem, he is not prepared to tell tales and admit that it was Bamforth who was causing trouble.

After the capture of the Japanese prisoner, none of the men is prepared to bayonet him, except, after a time-lapse, Bamforth, but it is Macleish who voices their official doubts in an exchange with Johnstone:

MACLEISH: You weren't in need of help. You cannot order men to put a bayonet in an unarmed prisoner.

JOHNSTONE: What do you think they dish you out with bayonets for? Just opening tins of soup?

MACLEISH: They're not to put in prisoners of war!

JOHNSTONE: You know what you can do with yours. You wouldn't know which end is which!

MACLEISH: If the need should arise, I'll use a bayonet with the next. But I've no intention of using one on any man who can't defend himself.

JOHNSTONE: You burk!
MACLEISH: He was a prisoner of war!
JOHNSTONE: Prisoner my crutch!
MACLEISH: There's such a thing as the Geneva Convention!

After Macleish and Smith have been out on reconnaissance patrol and have discovered that the Japanese army have broken through in their thousands, Macleish is clearly worried about his younger brother, Donald, who may be a prisoner of the Japanese. His train of thought leads him to look kindly on the prisoner, saying, 'He doesn't seem a bad sort of bloke.' He is clearly hoping that all Japanese soldiers are as decent as this one seems. It is Macleish who debates with Mitchem whether he has it in him to kill a man, whether knowing the enemy has a wife and family alters one's view of him, and what ultimately will happen to the prisoner. This is a very long conversation lasting ten pages of the play-text and is very revealing about both men. His worry about his brother perhaps being a prisoner makes him even more concerned about the fate of their Japanese prisoner, finishing with 'It's bloody murder, man!' Mitchem tries to make him see the reality of the situation by looking at the alternatives, finishing the conversation by saying, 'Before the month is out you'll do a dozen jobs like this before you have your breakfast. So just think on.'

By the end of the play, however, Macleish's attitude seems to have changed and is revealed when Bamforth appeals to him for help in preventing the prisoner from being killed. The stage-directions tell us that 'Macleish continues to stare out of the window,' and 'Macleish does not move.' Bamforth's reaction is stark. 'I hope they carve your brother up. Get that? I hope they carve your bloody brother up!'

How would you account for Macleish's change of heart towards the prisoner? Is he convinced by Mitchem's arguments, do you think, or is he taking the easy way out? Was his earlier insistence on the Geneva Convention merely an excuse for cowardice in the face of danger?

How would you sum up Macleish's character at the end of the play from all you have learnt of him? In professional terms, how would you rate his chances of promotion in the army? Would he make a good corporal and eventually a sergeant? Do you like him or dislike him?

WHITAKER

Whitaker is a private soldier who is responsible for the patrol's radio equipment. We very soon learn that he has been issued with an unreliable battery which means that the radio cannot contact base-camp. It was, presumably, his responsibility to check the battery before they left base which he has clearly failed to do. His incompetence makes him the butt of Bamforth's sarcasm. 'Now he tells us! Signals! Flipping signallers – I've shot 'em. Talk about the creek without a paddle.' Whitaker tries to make up for his incompetence by continuing to try to tune in the radio-set and is continually harassed by Bamforth. At first, therefore, the audience might feel sympathetic towards Whitaker, who, however incompetent he may have been, is trying hard to make amends. He seems young and vulnerable, so much so that he is protected by Mitchem against criticism by Johnstone.

In Act Two we get to know him a little better when the older men are teasing him about being young and inexperienced. Bamforth calls him 'The innocent abroad. The voice of experience.' Then comes the very touching story from Whitaker about his girlfriend who is 'bloody pretty, Smudge'. He says, ' . . . we had some smashing times together, me and her. I wish I was back there now, boy.' Smith listens quietly and sympathetically to this nostalgia and it is one of the quiet and moving episodes in the play, followed by Bamforth's sad song, 'A handsome young private lay dying'.

But there is the rather odd revelation too that Whitaker collects all kinds of Japanese army memorabilia – a fact he tries at first to deny. He does not explain why and it is left to us, the audience, to try to decide his motivation. Will he, when he returns home, try to pretend that he captured all of these war souvenirs from defeated Japanese soldiers? He seems embarrassed about this hobby as if it is something to be ashamed of.

He reveals himself as a very nervous and insecure young man when he is on guard-duty in Act Two and continually asks Mitchem the time. He clearly cannot be confident in this role of surveyor and is waiting to be relieved by another member of the patrol. It seems an uncharacteristic lapse on the part of Mitchem to give the sten-gun to Whitaker, who is so jumpy and nervous, and to ask him to cover the Japanese prisoner. It is clear that the slightest thing will unnerve Whitaker, and it does. His shooting of the prisoner is the signal for the deaths of all except Johnstone.

Whitaker is clearly the youngest and least experienced member of the patrol. How do you feel about him? Are you sorry that he is having to undergo such a terrifying experience or do you despise him for his incompetence?

Write a letter home to Mary, imagining that you are Whitaker and that you survive this patrol. What will you reveal and what will you hide about your feelings and actions during this time?

EVANS

Evans is a private soldier and is the target of much teasing by Bamforth because he is Welsh. He seems a simple, honest character who is genuinely amused by Bamforth's wit and turn of phrase. He sees the danger in Bamforth's continued taunting of Corporal Johnstone by warning him, 'Johnno's got it in for you, boyo. He'll have your guts for garters yet. He's after you. Chases you round from haircut to breakfast time.'

The audience is amused by Evans's pastime of reading his mother's women's magazine with its slushy, romantic serials especially when the magazines reach him in quite the wrong order, making the following of a serial impossible. His simplicity is shown in the enthusiasm with which he recounts the plot of these serials. However, this episode with Evans's magazine gives Bamforth the opportunity for a little more teasing and for Evans to philosophize about relationships between men and women before they are married. This, followed by

Evans's account of his girlfriend back in Wales, and his interest in Smith's family life establish him as basically a decent chap.

The stage-directions tell us that Evans is 'playfully sparring up to Bamforth' after being teased about his girlfriend running off with a Yank and this sparring ends with Evans having his ankle twisted until he confesses, 'I'm an ignorant Welsh Taff!' All of this is not a serious fight as is the later one between Bamforth and Macleish. Evans takes army life and all its banter with cheerfulness and good humour.

After Johnstone captures the Japanese prisoner, Evans, who is on guard-duty, is the first to confess that he cannot stick a bayonet into the prisoner. He does not philosophize later about it as does Macleish, he simply cannot kill a man. He shows kindness to the Japanese prisoner after Johnstone has torn up his photographs: 'Tojo . . . Tojo, boy. I got your pieces for you. You can stick them together again. Pot of paste and a bit of fiddling and they'll be right as rain.'

Look at page 77 where Evans tries to make everyone laugh by carrying out 'a "cod", guard mounting routine with exaggerated smartness'. Why, in your opinion, does he do this? Does this episode tell you anything about Evans?

What sort of man is Evans? Write down about five adjectives which you think describe his personality. What kind of relationship does he have with Bamforth?

BAMFORTH

Bamforth is a private soldier who establishes himself immediately as one who resents authority and is prepared to be insubordinate if he can get away with it. He is cheeky to Johnstone who orders him to his feet, moving slowly and asking, apparently innocently, 'You going to inspect us, Corp?' This cheekiness he practises on both Johnstone and Macleish but he draws the line at Mitchem who is more than a match for him. Mitchem calls him 'The barrack-room lawyer. The hard case.'

Not only is Bamforth witty and quick with his replies but he also sees himself as something of a fighter, showing his prowess in a tussle with Evans, a proposed fight with Macleish and, at the end of the play, a physical stand to protect the Japanese prisoner which ends in Mitchem striking Bamforth and Whitaker shooting the prisoner Unlike the other private soldiers, we hear little nostalgia from Bamforth; about his family, girlfriends or home life, although we can guess he comes from a deprived background when he talks about 'the London boys' if 'You ever want to see a bloke carved up'.

While Mitchem and Johnstone are out on their sortie at the beginning of the play, Bamforth's sarcasm, and even cruelty, annoys and bothers Whitaker, Smith and Macleish – almost to the point of fighting in the case of Macleish. Even the good-natured Evans, who tries sometimes to imitate Bamforth's wit, becomes annoyed with him. The men in the patrol are in a tense and dangerous situation and yet Bamforth increases the tension by taunting the others and getting on their nerves. His teasing makes the stress almost unbearable. All of them tell him to shut up.

We see a more likeable side of Bamforth in his friendship with Evans and the amusing episode of the 'Ladies Companion and Home'. His sparring with Evans is not malicious but more like two boys fighting. He has nothing to prove to Evans and does not have to match up to him as he does with Macleish and Johnstone. But it is in his relationship with the Japanese prisoner that the audience sees a more interesting side of Bamforth's character.

At first, when Bamforth is told by Mitchem to guard the prisoner, he treats the Japanese as if he is a performing animal which can be taught tricks. Bamforth may find it funny to speak in mock-Japanese and make the prisoner put his hands on and off his head, but to the audience this can appear as cruel behaviour to a pathetic and vulnerable prisoner. However, we see Bamforth warming to the man and being kind to him. Mitchem tells him, 'You're looking after Tojo here. I think he fancies you.' In the episode of the cigarettes when Bamforth is off-stage and Johnstone tears up the prisoner's photographs, Bamforth shows his humanity. 'You bastards.

You even had to rip his pictures up. You couldn't leave him them even!'

It takes Macleish a long time and a long talk with Mitchem to realize that the most realistic thing to do with the prisoner is to kill him. It takes Bamforth even longer to realize this. In fact, it does not occur to him that Mitchem plans to kill the prisoner until they have the argument about the water and then Johnstone puts it bluntly. 'He's stopping where he is. It's cobbler's for him.'

It is Bamforth who utters perhaps the most famous line in the play. To Johnstone's 'It's a bloody Nip,' Bamforth replies, 'He's a man!' Bamforth sees through the artificiality of war which makes men behave like animals and allows the Johnstones of this world power over others. He feels so strongly that he defends the life of the prisoner with his own life. He identifies with another victim and will not see him killed.

His last protest in the play is against the weakest member of the patrol, Whitaker, who brings about the deaths of nearly all of them. And then he is struck by Mitchem with the words, 'We've had enough from you.' Both Mitchem and Macleish have been through the same heart-searching which Bamforth is now exhibiting by his stand against them but they both realize that Bamforth's protection of the prisoner is unrealistic and potentially dangerous.

Why, do you think, is Bamforth the only one to try to save the prisoner? Would you have joined him or would you have done nothing? Explain your reasons.

Compare your attitude towards Bamforth at the end of Act Two with how you felt about him at the end of Act One. If it is significantly different, explain what has happened in Act Two to influence your opinion.

Do you think Bamforth's defence of the prisoner comes from the principles which Macleish professed earlier in the play or does it come from anger at authority? Imagine that you are Bamforth and have to explain your motivation at the end of the play. How would you explain yourself?

For many actors, the part of Bamforth is the most interesting and challenging in the play. Why do you think this is so? Would you like to play Bamforth?

SMITH

Smith is a private soldier somewhat older than the others and is the quietest and most reserved of them all. Bamforth gets on his nerves with his teasing and sarcasm and several times Smith tries to smooth the tension by telling Bamforth to shut up. He behaves as an older soldier would, and it is he who encourages Whitaker to tell the story of his love affair, asking questions so that Whitaker will go on talking. Whitaker has just been on guard-duty and has shown that he is very nervous and tense. Smith helps him to overcome his fear by talking about home.

We also hear about Smith's own home life. He is the only one of the patrol who has a wife and children and he tells the others about his life at home on the council estate: 'Made a sort of a bit of a lawn of it. Sit out on Sundays on it after dinner. Me and the missus.'

He is an ordinary man, caught up in the tensions and dangers of war, doing and saying nothing spectacular but simply another soldier to make up the requisite number on the patrol. He is like thousands of other men in the army. In this play, he does what he has to without arguing and avoids trouble. He protects Whitaker and shows him kindness.

Imagine you are Smith in this play. What thoughts and feelings do you have about the other members of your patrol? Which of the other men do you like best and why?

A JAPANESE SOLDIER

This is a difficult role to play even though he does not speak and does very little. He has to be a passive, vulnerable man who wins the compassion of the audience even though he is 'the enemy'. It is his very helplessness that arouses our sympathy. Some people in the audience may have opinions biased against the Japanese soldier because of their knowledge of the Second World War and the way some of the Japanese guards treated British and Allied prisoners of war. Younger members of the audience may have been swayed by the portrayal of the Japanese in films such as *The Bridge on the River Kwai* and *A Town Like Alice*.

He is the victim of war. Like the British soldiers he has been 'called up' into the army and, like them, is human and ordinary. He comes into the play because he has sneaked away from his own patrol to smoke a cigarette and by accident stumbles on to the path and the hut itself. He is the victim of Bamforth's sense of humour too, like the other characters, having to carry out childish tricks on command rather like a performing animal. But he shows a sense of comradeship, in spite of his situation, by offering his cigarettes around and by showing the photographs of his wife and family.

Our sympathy for him gradually grows as we witness the conversations between Macleish and Mitchem and between Johnstone and Mitchem about their prisoner's future. We feel for him when Johnstone cruelly tears up his photographs and threatens him. Our sympathy becomes anguish as his future is debated, especially when Bamforth tries to insist on giving the prisoner a drink, saying, 'He's not a camel!' This is another example of the device known as 'dramatic irony' by which the audience is allowed to know facts of which a character in the play is ignorant. Willis Hall uses it here to heighten our feelings about the prisoner.

His death seems inevitable especially when it is the nervous Whitaker who is ordered by Mitchem to 'Grab a gun and cover the Nip.' The prisoner does nothing to hasten his death except to stand up; it is Whitaker's panic which causes his death and, one could argue, the deaths of the others too.

Imagine that the Second Act ended differently and that you, as the Japanese prisoner, survived. Can you write your version of your brief imprisonment at the hands of the British patrol? What is your impression of each of the British soldiers? What is your explanation of your having a British cigarette-case? What are your feelings at the end of this experience?

Themes

MEN UNDER STRESS

The action of the play takes place in what most of us would regard as unnatural circumstances. Seven men are thrown together in time of war on a reconnaissance patrol in which it becomes clear that their lives are at stake. Apart from being members of this patrol and all soldiers in the British Army, they have no natural links of friendship. They have all been 'called up' and are therefore together against their will. This attitude is not voiced by all the members of the patrol, most of whom seem to accept the situation as inevitable. It is Bamforth who epitomizes the dissatisfaction which they all feel.

Bamforth does not accept the situation. He is positively aggressive and rude towards other members of the patrol, especially Johnstone. They are all in a dangerous situation and yet he makes the tension worse by arguing and bickering. These arguments occasionally lapse into fisticuffs which make the situation even more tense.

The tension stems not only from their perilous position, especially when it becomes clear that they are behind Japanese lines and thus cut off from their own main-base, but also from their individual worries and stress. For example, Mitchem has the responsibility of decisions for the whole patrol and the worry of how to get it back in what he realizes is an impossible situation. Whitaker has the worry of a useless radio-set and although he is responsible for communication with the outside world, in this he is a total failure. Macleish is worried about his younger brother, Donald, who is further up-county nearer the Japanese lines. All of these private worries are exaggerated by their predicament.

Their link with the outside world – the useless radio – provides yet more stress. It should be their life-line and yet a simple thing such as a dud battery means that they are stranded, without communication. In fact, the radio becomes exactly the opposite of hope and communication because its transmission betrays to the Japanese their exact position. At the end of Act One, the stage-direction reads that the Japanese operator's voice 'continues in taunting English'. The audience has suspected as much during Act One when Whitaker's attempts to 'raise' base-camp have ended in failure except in the trace of a Japanese voice. So they are isolated and apparently surrounded by the enemy whose whereabouts they can only guess at but who, apparently, know exactly where the British patrol is.

The acknowledgement of the hopelessness of their position cannot really be voiced. Mitchem has to try to cut through their stress and worry by offering them hope – the way out back to camp. The hut in which the patrol is hiding is both an escape from the war out there in the jungle and also a prison whose position has been pin-pointed by the Japanese. The realization of this reduces some of them to almost childlike dependence on Mitchem, for example Whitaker's constantly asking the time.

The stress of the situation is further complicated by the presence of the Japanese prisoner and the problem of what to do with him. Mitchem's original idea of trying to take him, alive, back to camp for the use he would be for information seems increasingly unrealistic. Both Mitchem and Johnstone realize that the man will have to be killed in order to safeguard their own lives but this apparently simple solution is complicated by Bamforth's defence of him. The playwright uses the technique of having one character in the play, Macleish, not understanding what is to become of the prisoner. Macleish can then question Mitchem, putting forward all the possibilities which are in the audience's mind too. This technique emphasizes the stress of the plot and involves the audience in the morality of killing the prisoner.

Since the essence of drama is conflict and conflict brings the worry and stress, it is clear that this play involves the characters in many kinds of stress. Stress results in arguing, fighting and, eventually, death. The audience is also involved with their problems because there are so many unanswered – perhaps unanswerable – questions!

COMRADESHIP

This patrol of seven men has been thrown together in the unnatural circumstances of war. At home in Britain they would have little in common because they are of different backgrounds, interests and temperaments. They have been conscripted into the army; they are not in Malaysia by their own choice. The play highlights the many tensions inherent in such a situation; indeed it seems that the members of this patrol spend much of their time squabbling. The fear which unites them into a kind of comradeship is the common fear of the enemy and of death.

They are united also because they are far away from home and their families, and, in this particular situation, far away from their base-camp which is near, geographically, but unreachable because of the Japanese forces surrounding them. Above all, they are unsure, inept and frightened. They have to put their trust in other soldiers such as Mitchem and Johnstone who are equally frightened.

From the horror of this situation the men take refuge in banter, teasing, grumbling and telling stories which all add up to the kind of comradeship which makes an unbearable situation bearable. There are no signs of deep or lasting friendships in this play but there is evidence of a common decency which in the end emphasizes the importance of individual men. Even Bamforth, who manages to annoy nearly all of the men in his patrol, finds a concerned colleague in Evans who tells him, 'Johnno's got it in for you, boyo. He'll have your guts for garters yet. He's after you. Chases you round from haircut to breakfast time.' And Mitchem too defends the apparently inept Whitaker against Johnstone by saying, 'It's not his fault. The battery's dis. OK, Sammy. Have another go. Better give it one more try.'

But most surprising of all is that the finest example of comradeship is that shown by Bamforth to the Japanese prisoner, something the audience would not have expected in the context of war. Willis Hall turns our expectations upside down.

When the Japanese soldier is first captured he is the anonymous 'enemy'. Both Bamforth and Johnstone are prepared to kill him with hardly a second thought. It is when the prisoner becomes a real human being with a wife and family that Bamforth befriends and defends him. Macleish, too, sees the prisoner in a different light, 'You hear all kinds of things. As if they're almost . . . animals. But this bloke seems a decent sort of bloke.' When the prospect of having to kill him seems a certainty we see the difference between the two extreme views.

JOHNSTONE: It's a bloody Nip.
BAMFORTH: He's a man!

DIGNITY

In his introduction to the play E. R. Wood tells us that, 'The author has said that the play is about human dignity.' The men in this play are in a situation where it is almost impossible to keep their dignity. Life in the army takes away all their privacy and discourages their capacity for independent thought and action. Because of this, they get on each other's nerves and their private worries and fears encourage squabbling and bickering.

In this play the characters are in a very frightening situation, apparently ambushed by the enemy with little chance of escape. It would be easy to lose one's dignity in such a situation, or as Bamforth puts it, 'suffering from screaming ab-dabs'. Army routine and the personality of Mitchem impose some kind of order on the patrol so that, in spite of some lapses, the men do retain their dignity.

But above all, it is the man who is most frightened and vulnerable, the Japanese prisoner, whose dignity commands our compassion and respect. He is outnumbered, a prisoner, not understanding the language and terrified of being killed and yet responds to overtures of friendship and returns them. Both Macleish and Bamforth defend him against ill-treatment and the possibility of being killed – which enhances them in our eyes.

GLOSSARY

Ab-dabs – hysterical fit
Al Capone – an American gangster of the 1920s
Barrackroom lawyer – a soldier who knows army regulations very well
Batt. – battery for the radio-transmitter
Bints – girls
Blanco – whitening for belts etc. in the army
Blighty – England, home
Blocks – stops
Bog – lavatory
Bonce – head
Book – army regulations
Bramah – attractive
Bucks – pounds
Buckshee – free gift
Bull – rubbish
Bundle – to be very keen on
Bungy – food
Burk – fool
Butcher's – look (rhyming slang: butcher's hook)
Call out the time – to be in charge, give orders
Cap and belt off – stripping a man of parts of his uniform before passing sentence in
  a Military Court
Carve up – to cheat, to kill
Case – examine closely
Charlie MacChan – Charlie Chan was a Chinese film detective
Chuff – to take no notice of
Civvy Street – civilian life, life after the army
CO – Commanding Officer (the Colonel)
Cobbler's – death
Cod – mock-American, as in a film-trailer
Come – insist on
Come it on – ask for trouble by behaving badly
Compo – abbreviation of 'composition': pack of food
Connor – food

Conshi – a conscientious objector, someone who will not fight

Cop – get or take

Creamer – a fool, mug

Creep – someone who flatters for favouritism

Crone – old woman (an insult)

Crumb – someone beneath notice (an insult)

Dancers – stairs or dance-hall

Detailed – ordered

Dis. – out of order

Ditched – left behind

Div. – an army division of about 12,000 soldiers

Do in or do for – kill

Doolally – stupid

Dose of salts – liver salts clear out the digestive system

Dracula – a monster in human shape who awakens at night and sucks the blood of young girls

Drag – a smoke

Drop one on – to strike or hit

Drum – lodging

Duff – useless

Eisteddfod – a Welsh assembly of poets and singers

Fatigues – army exercise

Fives – (page 5) five pound notes, (page 75) fists

Fix – to locate a position

Fred Karno's mob – a useless bunch of soldiers, called after a comedian famous for portraying incompetence

Geisha girls or fillies – Japanese dancing-girls or escorts

Gelt – money, gold

Geneva Convention – an agreement under which prisoners of war were to be humanely treated

Get – an abusive term for a man

Get fell in – to stand to attention as if for inspection

Gillo – hurry

Ginks – an abusive term for men

Give us the heels together – an order to stand to attention

Graft – work

Gripe – complain

Haggis – a distinctive Scottish dish

Haircut to breakfast time – all the time

Half-inch – steal (rhymes with 'pinch')

Happen – perhaps

Hard case – a difficult man to deal with

Henry Hall – a conductor of dance-music on the radio

Herb – an abusive term for a man

Hump – blow

Humpy – army back-pack

I/C – in charge

Jack it in – stop doing something

Jack the Ripper – a Victorian multi-murderer

Joan of Arc – fifteenth-century French peasant girl who 'heard voices' telling her to lead the army against the English

Johnee – an Englishman

Joskins – new, inexperienced soldiers

King's Regs – King's Regulations sets out the legal duties and obligations of army personnel

Kip – sleep

Knotted, get knotted – an insult

Kybosh – to put a stop to

Lacas – be quick

Land's End to How's Your Father – over the whole country

Lay me odds – have a bet with me

Lingo – language

Madame Butterfly – a Japanese character in the opera by Puccini

Marconi – an early inventor in the history of radio

Muckers – friends

Mugs away – the losers of the last game of darts begin the next one

NAAFI – Navy, Army and Air Force Institutes – canteens

NCO – Non-commissioned officer

Nip, Nippo – Japanese

Nub – cigarette

Once over – look closely at

PBI – poor, bloody infantry

Pull – plead or insist on

Rising Sun – the Japanese flag

Rita Hayworth – beautiful film star of the 1930s and 1940s

Roll on – hope it ends soon

Rookie – new soldier, raw recruit

RSM – Regimental Sergeant-Major

Sarge and Sarnt – abbreviation of Sergeant

Saw you coming – you are easily fooled

Scarper – run away

Shouting the odds – showing off

Shufti – take a look

Shun – abbreviation for 'attention'

Skin and blister – sister (rhyming slang)

Skive – get out of something

Snappers – children

Snout – cigarette

SOB – son of a bitch

Sortie – reconnaissance

Spout – rifle breech

Stag – sentry duty, lookout

Straight up – it's the truth

Swag – stolen loot

Swallow – smoke

Tapes – stripes indicating authority – one for a lance-corporal, two for a corporal and three for a sergeant

Tod – alone

Tojo – any Japanese, from the Japanese Prime Minister during the Second World War

Tripes – insides

Two's up – next in turn

U J Club – Union Jack Club

U/S – unserviceable, useless

Rudolph Valentino – handsome star of the silent films

Wallahs – self-important men

Whipped – stolen

Wog – an insulting term for any foreigner

W O Is – Warrant Officers, 1st class

Wonky – out of order

Yellow peril – threat from the East

Discussion Topics, Activities and GCSE Examination Questions

DISCUSSION TOPICS

Your understanding and appreciation of the play will be much increased if you discuss aspects of it with other people. Here are some topics you could consider:

1.   Willis Hall has said that this play is about human dignity. Do you feel that war is a dignifying or a degrading experience?

2.   Does the end of this play result from man's strengths or his weaknesses?

3.   Do you think that in all civilizations war is inevitable?

4.   Could you imagine this play set in another quite different war? What changes would you have to make?

5.   Stress sometimes destroys people and sometimes causes them to act in an exaggerated – even heroic – way. What effect does stress have in this play?

6.   In the introduction to this play, on page ix, we are told, 'The Author has said that the play is about human dignity.' What is dignity? Which of the characters, in your opinion, retain their dignity and which do not?

7.   Who is the most important character in this play, in your view? Defend your opinion by using specific evidence from the text.

8.   If you could play any character in this play, which one would you choose and why?

ACTIVITIES

1.   Imagine that the patrol lives through this reconnaissance mission and that back at base Bamforth is court-martialled because of his attack on Johnstone. Write out Mitchem's report of what happened.

2.　Imagine that you are the lawyer asked to represent Bamforth at his court-martial. What would be your main arguments in his defence?

3.　Make up your own story or play about Bamforth *before* the events in this play, trying to keep the same characteristics of personality and speech-patterns as in Willis Hall's play.

4.　Continue the play, describing how a Japanese patrol enters the hut and finds Johnstone wounded and attempting to surrender. What happens next?

5.　Look again at the end of Act One and the beginning of Act Two. There is a half-hour interval. With a group, improvise what happens in the hut in that time.

6.　Rewrite this play as a short story keeping the main events and the same characters.

7.　With a group, discuss what you think is the funniest part of the play, the most exciting, the most dramatic, and the saddest.

8.　Produce a TV news report on what happened to Mitchem's patrol in the jungle.

9.　Make a map of the Malayan peninsula showing the position of Singapore, the route taken by Mitchem's patrol and the advance of the Japanese army.

10.　The CO back at base-camp – if he lived through the Japanese attack – would have the very sad task of writing to the families back in Britain informing them of the deaths of the members of the patrol. Write one or more of these letters, remembering that in a letter of condolence the writer is always kind about the dead person.

11.　Either in discussion in a group or in writing try to decide what each of the men in the patrol would do as a job in 'Civvy Street'.

12.　In a group try a 'role-play' exercise where one of you imagines himself or herself to be one of the characters at a specific moment in the play. Stay in character while the other members of the group question you about your hopes, background, opinions, relationships, motivation and so on.

13.　Imagine that you are the headteachers of each of the men in the British patrol when they were at school. Write their school-leaving reports.

14.　The radio-operator back at base will have heard the last few minutes of this play and whatever happens next. Imagine you are this radio-operator and write out your report for your CO.

15.   On pages 42 and 43, Mitchem and Johnstone argue about whether or not to kill the prisoner. Imagine that one of them does kill the prisoner and that the patrol survives. Write out a report as if you are Mitchem for your Commanding Officer back a. base stating clearly the reasons for your decision. You will need to be persuasive but truthful.

GCSE EXAMINATION QUESTIONS

In this examination you may find that the set texts have been selected by your teacher from a very wide list of titles in the examination syllabus. The questions in the examination paper will therefore be applicable to many different books. Here are some questions which you could answer by making use of *The Long and the Short and the Tall*.

1.   Select a book or play in which the characters find themselves in danger. What effect does this situation have on the way they behave?

2.   Write about a character in a play or novel who is at first disliked by the reader or audience but who then redeems himself so that he is admired. What techniques does the novelist or playwright use to bring about this change?

3.   Choose a novel or a play in which we gradually grow to like the characters the more we know about their backgrounds and opinions. How is this information conveyed to us?

4.   Write about a character in a play or novel who is clearly a leader of a group of people. What are the particular qualities of leadership in the character you have chosen and how are these qualities shown to us?

5.   Have you read a book or play in which there is one apparent trouble-maker? What effect does this character have on the development of the story?

FOR THE BEST IN PAPERBACKS, LOOK FOR THE

In every corner of the world, on every subject under the sun, Penguin represents quality and variety – the very best in publishing today.

For complete information about books available from Penguin – including Pelicans, Puffins, Peregrines and Penguin Classics – and how to order them, write to us at the appropriate address below. Please note that for copyright reasons the selection of books varies from country to country.

In the United Kingdom: For a complete list of books available from Penguin in the U.K., please write to *Dept E.P., Penguin Books Ltd, Harmondsworth, Middlesex, UB7 0DA*

In the United States: For a complete list of books available from Penguin in the U.S., please write to *Dept BA, Penguin, 299 Murray Hill Parkway, East Rutherford, New Jersey 07073*

In Canada: For a complete list of books available from Penguin in Canada, please write to *Penguin Books Canada Ltd, 2801 John Street, Markham, Ontario L3R 1B4*

In Australia: For a complete list of books available from Penguin in Australia, please write to the *Marketing Department, Penguin Books Australia Ltd, P.O. Box 257, Ringwood, Victoria 3134*

In New Zealand: For a complete list of books available from Penguin in New Zealand, please write to the *Marketing Department, Penguin Books (NZ) Ltd, Private Bag, Takapuna, Auckland 9*

In India: For a complete list of books available from Penguin, please write to *Penguin Overseas Ltd, 706 Eros Apartments, 56 Nehru Place, New Delhi, 110019*

In Holland: For a complete list of books available from Penguin in Holland, please write to *Penguin Books Nederland B.V., Postbus 195, NL–1380AD Weesp, Netherlands*

In Germany: For a complete list of books available from Penguin, please write to *Penguin Books Ltd, Friedrichstrasse 10 – 12, D–6000 Frankfurt Main 1, Federal Republic of Germany*

In Spain: For a complete list of books available from Penguin in Spain, please write to *Longman Penguin España, Calle San Nicolas 15, E–28013 Madrid, Spain*

PENGUIN CLASSICS

Netochka Nezvanova Fyodor Dostoyevsky

Dostoyevsky's first book tells the story of 'Nameless Nobody' and introduces many of the themes and issues which will dominate his great masterpieces.

Selections from the Carmina Burana A verse translation by David Parlett

The famous songs from the *Carmina Burana* (made into an oratorio by Carl Orff) tell of lecherous monks and corrupt clerics, drinkers and gamblers, and the fleeting pleasures of youth.

Fear and Trembling Søren Kierkegaard

A profound meditation on the nature of faith and submission to God's will which examines with startling originality the story of Abraham and Isaac.

Selected Prose Charles Lamb

Lamb's famous essays (under the strange pseudonym of Elia) on anything and everything have long been celebrated for their apparently innocent charm; this major new edition allows readers to discover the darker and more interesting aspects of Lamb.

The Picture of Dorian Gray Oscar Wilde

Wilde's superb and macabre novella, one of his supreme works, is reprinted here with a masterly Introduction and valuable Notes by Peter Ackroyd.

A Treatise of Human Nature David Hume

A universally acknowledged masterpiece by 'the greatest of all British Philosophers' – A. J. Ayer

FOR THE BEST IN PAPERBACKS, LOOK FOR THE

PENGUIN CLASSICS

A Passage to India   E. M. Forster

Centred on the unresolved mystery in the Marabar Caves, Forster's great work provides the definitive evocation of the British Raj.

The Republic   Plato

The best-known of Plato's dialogues, *The Republic* is also one of the supreme masterpieces of Western philosophy whose influence cannot be overestimated.

The Life of Johnson   James Boswell

Perhaps the finest 'life' ever written, Boswell's *Johnson* captures for all time one of the most colourful and talented figures in English literary history.

Remembrance of Things Past (3 volumes)   Marcel Proust

This revised version by Terence Kilmartin of C. K. Scott Moncrieff's original translation has been universally acclaimed – available for the first time in paperback.

Metamorphoses   Ovid

A golden treasury of myths and legends which has proved a major influence on Western literature.

A Nietzsche Reader   Friedrich Nietzsche

A superb selection from all the major works of one of the greatest thinkers and writers in world literature, translated into clear, modern English.

FOR THE BEST IN PAPERBACKS, LOOK FOR THE 🐧

PENGUIN CLASSICS

John Aubrey	**Brief Lives**
Francis Bacon	**The Essays**
James Boswell	**The Life of Johnson**
Sir Thomas Browne	**The Major Works**
John Bunyan	**The Pilgrim's Progress**
Edmund Burke	**Reflections on the Revolution in France**
Thomas de Quincey	**Confessions of an English Opium Eater**
	Recollections of the Lakes and the Lake Poets
Daniel Defoe	**A Journal of the Plague Year**
	Moll Flanders
	Robinson Crusoe
	Roxana
	A Tour Through the Whole Island of Great Britain
Henry Fielding	**Jonathan Wild**
	Joseph Andrews
	The History of Tom Jones
Oliver Goldsmith	**The Vicar of Wakefield**
William Hazlitt	**Selected Writings**
Thomas Hobbes	**Leviathan**
Samuel Johnson/	**A Journey to the Western Islands of**
James Boswell	**Scotland/The Journal of a Tour to the**
	Hebrides
Charles Lamb	**Selected Prose**
Samuel Richardson	**Clarissa**
	Pamela
Adam Smith	**The Wealth of Nations**
Tobias Smollet	**Humphry Clinker**
Richard Steele and	Selections from the **Tatler** and the **Spectator**
Joseph Addison	
Laurence Sterne	**The Life and Opinions of Tristram Shandy,**
	Gentleman
	A Sentimental Journey Through France and Italy
Jonathan Swift	**Gulliver's Travels**
Dorothy and William	**Home at Grasmere**
Wordsworth	

Matthew Arnold	**Selected Prose**
Jane Austen	**Emma**
	Lady Susan, The Watsons, Sanditon
	Mansfield Park
	Northanger Abbey
	Persuasion
	Pride and Prejudice
	Sense and Sensibility
Anne Brontë	**The Tenant of Wildfell Hall**
Charlotte Brontë	**Jane Eyre**
	Shirley
	Villette
Emily Brontë	**Wuthering Heights**
Samuel Butler	**Erewhon**
	The Way of All Flesh
Thomas Carlyle	**Selected Writings**
Wilkie Collins	**The Moonstone**
	The Woman in White
Charles Darwin	**The Origin of Species**
Charles Dickens	**American Notes for General Circulation**
	Barnaby Rudge
	Bleak House
	The Christmas Books
	David Copperfield
	Dombey and Son
	Great Expectations
	Hard Times
	Little Dorrit
	Martin Chuzzlewit
	The Mystery of Edwin Drood
	Nicholas Nickleby
	The Old Curiosity Shop
	Oliver Twist
	Our Mutual Friend
	The Pickwick Papers
	Selected Short Fiction
	A Tale of Two Cities

Benjamin Disraeli	**Sybil**
George Eliot	**Adam Bede**
	Daniel Deronda
	Felix Holt
	Middlemarch
	The Mill on the Floss
	Romola
	Scenes of Clerical Life
	Silas Marner
Elizabeth Gaskell	**Cranford** and **Cousin Phillis**
	The Life of Charlotte Brontë
	Mary Barton
	North and South
	Wives and Daughters
Edward Gibbon	**The Decline and Fall of the Roman Empire**
George Gissing	**New Grub Street**
Edmund Gosse	**Father and Son**
Richard Jefferies	**Landscape with Figures**
Thomas Macaulay	**The History of England**
Henry Mayhew	**Selections from London Labour** and **The London Poor**
John Stuart Mill	**On Liberty**
William Morris	**News from Nowhere** and **Selected Writings and Designs**
Walter Pater	**Marius the Epicurean**
John Ruskin	**'Unto This Last' and Other Writings**
Sir Walter Scott	**Ivanhoe**
Robert Louis Stevenson	**Dr Jekyll and Mr Hyde**
William Makepeace Thackeray	**The History of Henry Esmond**
	Vanity Fair
Anthony Trollope	**Barchester Towers**
	Framley Parsonage
	Phineas Finn
	The Warden
Mrs Humphrey Ward	**Helbeck of Bannisdale**
Mary Wollstonecraft	**Vindication of the Rights of Woman**

Arnold Bennett	**The Old Wives' Tale**
Joseph Conrad	**Heart of Darkness**
	Nostromo
	The Secret Agent
	The Shadow-Line
	Under Western Eyes
E. M. Forster	**Howard's End**
	A Passage to India
	A Room With a View
	Where Angels Fear to Tread
Thomas Hardy	**The Distracted Preacher and Other Tales**
	Far From the Madding Crowd
	Jude the Obscure
	The Mayor of Casterbridge
	The Return of the Native
	Tess of the d'Urbervilles
	The Trumpet Major
	Under the Greenwood Tree
	The Woodlanders
Henry James	**The Aspern Papers and The Turn of the Screw**
	The Bostonians
	Daisy Miller
	The Europeans
	The Golden Bowl
	An International Episode and Other Stories
	Portrait of a Lady
	Roderick Hudson
	Washington Square
	What Maisie Knew
	The Wings of the Dove
D. H. Lawrence	**The Complete Short Novels**
	The Plumed Serpent
	The Rainbow
	Selected Short Stories
	Sons and Lovers
	The White Peacock
	Women in Love

FOR THE BEST IN PAPERBACKS, LOOK FOR THE

PENGUIN REFERENCE BOOKS

The Penguin Guide to the Law

This acclaimed reference book is designed for everyday use, and forms the most comprehensive handbook ever published on the law as it affects the individual.

The Penguin Medical Encyclopedia

Covers the body and mind in sickness and in health, including drugs, surgery, history, institutions, medical vocabulary and many other aspects. 'Highly commendable' – *Journal of the Institute of Health Education*

The Penguin French Dictionary

This invaluable French-English, English-French dictionary includes both the literary and dated vocabulary needed by students, and the up-to-date slang and specialized vocabulary (scientific, legal, sporting, etc) needed in everyday life. As a passport to the French language, it is second to none.

A Dictionary of Literary Terms

Defines over 2,000 literary terms (including lesser known, foreign language and technical terms) explained with illustrations from literature past and present.

The Penguin Map of Europe

Covers all land eastwards to the Urals, southwards to North Africa and up to Syria, Iraq and Iran. Scale – 1:5,500,000, 4-colour artwork. Features main roads, railways, oil and gas pipelines, plus extra information including national flags, currencies and populations.

The Penguin Dictionary of Troublesome Words

A witty, straightforward guide to the pitfalls and hotly disputed issues in standard written English, illustrated with examples and including a glossary of grammatical terms and an appendix on punctuation.

FOR THE BEST IN PAPERBACKS, LOOK FOR THE

PENGUIN PASSNOTES

This comprehensive series, designed to help O-level, GCSE and CSE students, includes:

SUBJECTS
Biology
Chemistry
Economics
English Language
Geography
Human Biology
Mathematics
Modern Mathematics
Modern World History
Narrative Poems
Nursing
Physics

SHAKESPEARE
As You Like It
Henry IV, Part I
Henry V
Julius Caesar
Macbeth
The Merchant of Venice
A Midsummer Night's Dream
Romeo and Juliet
Twelfth Night

LITERATURE
Arms and the Man
Cider With Rosie
Great Expectations
Jane Eyre
Kes
Lord of the Flies
A Man for All Seasons
The Mayor of Casterbridge
My Family and Other Animals
Pride and Prejudice
The Prologue to The Canterbury
　Tales
Pygmalion
Saint Joan
She Stoops to Conquer
Silas Marner
To Kill a Mockingbird
War of the Worlds
The Woman in White
Wuthering Heights